T0104010

THE PEACEFUL COMBATANT

A BLOODY CONFLICT THROUGH THE EYES OF A PEACEKEEPER

SANYA AINA

Order this book online at www.trafford.com
or email orders@trafford.com

Most Trafford titles are also available at major online book retailers.

Print information available on the last page.

ISBN: 978-1-4907-6860-1 (sc)
ISBN: 978-1-4907-6859-5 (e)

Trafford rev. 05/27/2016

Trafford
PUBLISHING® www.trafford.com

North America & international
toll-free: 1 888 232 4444 (USA & Canada)
fax: 812 355 4082

The night air was very humid and warm, the ceiling fan breeze provided the only source of cool breeze that enabled me fall asleep beside Ajuma my wife, who also was fast asleep. I was woken up by the sound of the beagle which signified an emergency parade has been ordered,

As I struggled to gain full consciousness, my mind started to ponder over what might have necessitated the parade. Has a coup d'état taken place, what could have happened in such an odd hour of the day, I leaned over to see if Ajuma has also been awoken by the sound of the beagle but she was still deeply asleep, what an innocent pretty Angel I thought.

Ajuma is a lady I considered the most humble, caring, loving wife, yet beautiful by all standard, I believe she is a priceless gift God has ever given me, I got married to her just five months ago when I visited my village in the middle belt region of Nigeria, in what was a very low keyed ceremony, it was barely two years after my enlistment into the Nigeria army. After my six months recruitment training in Zaria, Kaduna state of Nigeria, I was drafted to the 149 Battalion of the Nigeria Army based in Lagos Nigeria.

My parents had objected bitterly to my joining the Army with all means at their disposal but I remained adamant about my decision. Five years after my secondary school education, I was unable to further my education due to paucity of fund and getting a job that could support me and my ageing parents and younger ones, I became so frustrated that I once contemplated suicide as a way out of my predicament, just when I thought all hope was lost, came this recruitment advertisement published in several Nigeria newspapers, without hesitation, I jumped at the offer as I possessed all but one of the requirement, the heart to kill.

However, I am now a conscripted soldier, after going through what seemed like six months sojourn in the kingdom of Hell.

Ajuma remained in a deep sleep despite the loud sound of the beagle, I tried all I could not to disturb her sleep, activities of the past day may have had a heavy toll on her, I quietly got off the bed and reached for my tooth brush and paste, after cleaning up, I put on my military camouflage, hurriedly laced my black shinny combat boot and was fully geared up to join several of my colleagues whose footsteps are loudly pounding toward the parade ground.

I quietly tip toed to my bed side to see my lovely Angel still fast asleep, I stood and watched her for several minutes praying silently that I should never have the reason to leave her, thoughts of when I deflowered her flashed across my mind, I bent over and kissed her partly opened lip softly, she groan slightly and continued sleeping, what an innocent perfect beauty, I thought. I silently moved toward the exit of my tiny one room apartment that Ajuma was so happy to share with me despite all the odds. I stepped outside as quietly as I could and shut the door.

I got to the parade ground sweating profusely because I had to jog to get there on time to meet up with my comrades, we hurriedly assembled and stood at attention, after several minutes of parade and drills presided over by the Parade Commander, He addressed us briefly, he told us that the battalion had received a signal from the Defence Headquarter to assemble the battalion for an emergency operation and that the General Officer Commanding (GOC) will arrive in a short while to elaborate on the content of the signal.

The men of the149 Battalion remained at ease on the parade ground till 10:00hrs, yet there was no sign of the GOC, the day had begun to warm up due to the intense heat from the sun, soon the weather began to have its toll on us, to comfort myself, I briefly allowed my mind to drift toward Ajuma, I began to ponder what we would be doing together if I were to be with her, I assume by now my breakfast of corn cereal will be ready and waiting to be consumed. I thought.

By 13:23hrs I spotted the convoy of the GOC approaching the parade ground, we've been scorched by the heat of the sun for over seven hours. Suddenly, I was jolted by a sound which stopped my day dreaming abruptly, the GOC inspected the parade briefly and he then went ahead to give us the full detail of the reason of the our emergency parade.

After the GOC's twenty three minutes address which detailed that our battalion had been assigned to Sierra Leone with immediate effect to be part of a multi-national Economic Community of West Africa Peace Keeping Force, simply known as ECOMOG.

Our mission, we were told was to enforce peace and normalcy in Sierra Leone and that our mission had the blessing of the UN and the international community. He explained further that the military forces in Sierra Leone has been polarized thereby leading to the partial collapse of military forces.

At the end of the GOC's address, we were ordered to match to the armoury to sign for our rifle and ammunitions, I still can't believe that I'm about to leave my sweet angel so suddenly without even saying good bye, and heading to another man's country to fight another man's fight. What if I didn't make it back alive? How long will I be staying away without seeing Ajuma? These and other thoughts filled my mind, I felt very sorry for Ajuma, why did I joined the Army? I wondered, I began to blame myself for not listening to my parents warning to stay away from military profession.

During my rifle and ammunition signing procedures, I quickly scribble a few line for Ajuma on a piece of paper I found in my pocket, I promised I will not be away for long and that after a week or two I will be back, what if this deployment last longer than two week, what will I do? I thought, perhaps, I will just abscond, quit the army for good and be with her, together we can find other means of livelihood, these thoughts raced through my mind.

Before our departure I made concrete arrangement for Ajuma to get seventy five percent of my monthly salary for her up keep and I pleaded with my elder brother to always help check on her wellbeing, pending my return from this unfortunate and unexpected assignment that didn't give me the opportunity to tell the love of my life good bye.

After we had finished signing and double checking our weapons, several huge military personnel carrier trucks were assigned to convey the battalion to the only international airport in Lagos. The Muritala Mohammed International Airport Lagos. The trip to the airport was characterized by vehicular gridlock, due to the nature of the heavy traffic on Lagos road, other motorist tried as much as possible to avoid our military convoy knowing what the consequence of running into a military vehicle would be.

The waiting game continued on till 23:45hrs when a huge Lockheed Hercules C130 military transport plane rolled to sight on the tarmac of Muritala Mohammed International Airport in Ikeja Lagos, it is the aircraft we've all being waiting for to airlift us to Sierra Leone to join the Ecomog peace keeping troops.

Within three hours, the entire 149 battalion have completed all the necessary procedure of getting on board the plane, and in no time we were all on board the C130 plane with all our military hardware.

As the flight commenced, I recalled that it is my first ever flight, I went through all the strange psychological experience, but my mind never drifted away from Ajuma, I prayed that I survive this mission and return alive and well to Ajuma and maybe resign from the army, because Ajuma was more important to me than the Nigeria Army.

About an hour into the flight, the flight crew announced we were approaching Lungi international Airport, Lungi is a coastal town close to Freetown Sierra Leone capital, and the Airport itself was the former operational base of the British Royal Air force. The runway is about 10,488 ft. In length and it's made of asphalt.

A few moment later, the pilot announced his inability to land the plane due to the relentless shelling of the airport by the Revolutionary United Front popularly called the RUF, the pilot went further to explain that he's doing everything possible to land the plane safely.

Looking out of the plane's opening I saw flashes of light brighten the darkness below at intervals, my heart kept pounding hard against my chest, if the plane is hit by a rocket propelled grenade or a shrapnel? Ajuma will never see me again, my parent will always blame me for joining the army due to lack of job opportunity, if I am killed in this peacekeeping adventure. How will my parents cope with the news of my demise, I thought. I wondered and started praying to God to deliver me from this calamity that is trying to befall me.

I again strained my eyes to look downward, I saw sparks of fire, like the sparks from a cigarette lighter, the shelling was relentless, what if the entire airport is destroyed, how would the pilot land this plane safely? I thought. We flew for another hour cycling the less hostile areas, occasionally, I peeped through the plane's window to see if the shelling has subsided but the sparks of light continued unabated.

Thirty minutes later the worst happened, the pilot announced that he has been using the reserve fuel, that the plane was scheduled for just two hours thirty minute flight to Freetown.

I wondered how the government could be so careless about its personnel, what will it cost the military authority to fuel this transport plane adequately, but they failed to, instead, they choose to put our lives at risk for personal gain. Now we will all perish, if this plane should be forced to land amid this fierce shelling,

When I looked through the opening of the plane, the sparks still appeared vivid, for a moment I thought of jumping out of the flying plane, I preferred to die alone than be consumed by fire in a burning aircraft. Somehow, I managed to remain calm and prayed harder for God's timely intervention.

Ten minutes later the pilot announced he would be landing the plane despite the continuous bombardment on the ground, he further explained that the plane would crash land if it ran out of fuel, he urged us to brace up and pray for a safe landing.

We all started praying in choruses and for the first time I saw some of my colleagues I have considered ungodly prayed fervently to God to save their lives.

At some point I didn't bother peeping through the plane's window anymore but I kept my prayers steadily flowing to God for compassion. How could Ajuma loss me just because I want to enforce peace in senseless war.

The massive C130 plane surged downward starting its landing attempt, the downward surge jolted us awake from our fervent prayers and silence suddenly enveloped the belly of the huge plane, only the roar of the gigantic engine remained audible.

After series of jerks and plunges, the plane surged forward just then I saw a red hot metallic object, the size of a beer bottle whisked by, missing my side of the plane's window by a few inches. I felt frightened, everyone in the plane looked stone dead already, moments went by, and all of a sudden a voice blared through the public address system of the plane announcing that we were going to attempt another landing, the pilot didn't hide the fact that the plane was seriously low on fuel and we should all brace up for the worst.

The plane made a right turn and surged downward, the experience reminded me of a rough roller coaster ride I once had. I tighten my grip on the rail close to me, I closed my eyes so tight as if it will make me vanish from the plane bell and reappear beside Ajuma. that was what my imagination was.

The plane continued its downward surge while the sound of exploding ordnance became even louder. The loud noise of the explosions interrupted whatever silence we had previously enjoyed. Miraculously, the plane was not hit by any explosive device. As we continued our downward plunge I felt the plane hit the surface of the airport asphalt runway, we all yelled at the top of our voices not knowing what that shout was for, I exhaled aloud and started praying that our plane should not be hit by explosives.

After what seemed like eternity, the plane's bell rested on a section of the runway of the Lungi International Airport in one piece. A brief moment of silence was presided by a shout for joy, thanking God for sparing our live and not allowing the plane to be blown into bits in mid-air by the shelling of the airport.

When the jubilation subsided, the sound of explosion that had earlier enveloped the airport also became calm. Our Commander, Army Major, Ojo Yusuf, ordered twenty five of my colleagues to get ready to disembark from the plane, their mission he explained was to safeguard the surrounding of the plane for the rest of the battalion and for our hardware to safely disembark, Major Ojo barked out his strategies to the selected soldiers, when he had finished dolling out the orders, the men took strategic positions in front of the plane's main exit ready for action.

Major Ojo reached for a communication device installed in the plane and ordered the Pilot to open the plane's main exit, as the door swung open slowly the smell of burning substance filtered into the plane. The men slowly eased out of the plane with their AK47 rifle firmly in their hands and pointing ahead of them.

Just as the last soldier eased out of sight, I heard the outburst of machine gun firing rapidly and an outburst of cry for help, I held my breath briefly, as one of the soldier outside the plane shouted that the RUF rebels had surrounded the plane Major Ojo yelled out "Ibrahim," the name of one of the soldier who had earlier disembarked several times but got no response. Major Ojo looked confused realizing that we've been trapped by the dreaded RUF Rebel.

When the machine gun fire died down briefly, I peeped outside the plane opening and saw nothing but pitch darkness. I didn't see any rebels and yet the RUF rebels were said to have surrounded us, I tightened my grip on my rifle and wondered if all of my twenty five colleagues had been killed or struggling to stay alive.

Major Ojo, hurriedly assembled another thirty men and passed instruction to them. He wanted the men to disembark and check out what the situation outside the plane was like, but this time, the men will use another of the plane emergency exit.

The men match toward the direction of the C130 exit, this time the door was hesitantly opened and they quickly eased out of the plane but as the last man dropped out of sight there was another outburst of machine gun fire that lasted much longer than the earlier one, after a while, silence enveloped the surrounding area, and without any word from our men outside the plane.

The Assistant Commander Lieutenant Johnson west, approached Major Ojo and they discussed for about ten minutes then Major Ojo headed for the cockpit area and soon disappeared. We've not been able to establish any radio contact with our comrades outside, Lieut. Johnson said. Even Members the ECOMOG forces on ground are still not talking to us yet He stressed in frustration. I assumed the friendly forces on ground should have been informed prior to our departure, why were we not getting any assistant, I wondered.

The siege continued for several hours, without any knowledge of our fate, the day's brightness began to gradually fade away while darkness started to crawl in as the siege continued'

By 6:25am the next day, there was another outburst of machine gun fire, the latest in spike, with the sounds of grenade and mortar explosions. Just when all hope had faded in the barrage of blasts, the Ghanaian and Guinean ECOMOG contingents are on their way to help us loosen the grip on the airport, Major Ojo yelled as he hastily exited the cockpit of the big plane. Everyone should be ready to get off this plane soon, he continued.

The sound of explosions and machine gun fire continued intensively outside the plane as we all braced up and awaited the disembarkment order, i remained baffled by the miraclous way the huge plane escape been hit by explosions and shrepnel, but i could hear bullets hitting the massive body of the plane repeatedly.

Daylight had swept away the darkness completly as i appraoched closest window to me and peeped through, i saw the layout of Lungi Airport in the clear morning light, my attention was suddenly drawn by military camouflage uniforms litering that side of the plane, wow! I exclaimed, so the rebels RUF had killed our men, i thought.

I quickly closed my eyes briefly and prrayed fervently for the first time. Absoluted fear griped my mind and i wished everything i saw then were mere dreams, but ironically it was stack reality, when i open my eyes to stare again i noticed a group of advancing soliders with ECOMOG emblem on thier uniforms, they were approaching the plane from the side of my position, somehow i managd to remain silent.

The Ecomog troops advanced very rapidly from my side of view and soon they succeded in securing my side of the plane firmly, "advance ten at a time from the west side of the plane," was the next word i heard blaring out of the plane's public address system, as if i was looking for a missing object on the ground, i sneaked to the back of the plane and joined the last ten soldiers to exit the plane's belly, amidst an horrific fear that griped me, I patently awaited my turn to alight.

Just fresh from recruitment deport I had no actual combat experience and here I am face to face with the worst fear of my live. The soldiers started disembarking gently as planned, with intermitted scream very audible from where I stood, my heart kept pounding vigorously.

The explosions been heard around us eased slightly leaving the cracking sound of machine gun fire to predominantly fill the air. About half of the military contingent had left the plane, which gave us the hope that the surrounding of the plane had been secured.

Stoppage order was issued for the rest soldiers to stay on board so I remained on board the plane, wishing not to venture of out the plane.

The troops on ground engaged the RUF rebels in a fierce gun battle for the control of the airport, the troops were assisted by other ECOMOG contingent. After a long wait it became apparent that the soldiers had succeeded in pushing the rebels backward and out of the Lungi International Airport.

''I want everyone out of this plane,'' Major Ojo shouted out as he emerged out of the plane's cockpit. I became the last soldier to leave the plane, as I stepped down I uttered yet more prayers to God to save my soul. The last batch of soldiers to leave the plane which I was one of them got the order to recover all our casualties and put them back on board the plane. I have never touched an actual dead person before but that was about to change now I muttered.

I hung my rifle securely behind my back and paired with a fellow soldier to carry out the order. Just a few yards away lay three bullet ridden bodies of my colleague i knew so well. The rebels had succeeded in killing the entire first batch of soldiers that disembarked from the plane. I thought, as we walked toward the three motionless bodies.

I beefed up my courage and took a very deep breath when we reached the spot where the dead soldiers laid. I grabbed the upper arm of one of the dead men and dragged him toward the plane's entrance, my colleague somehow lifted the other corpse on his shoulder and carried the dead man into the plane with much more ease than I did.

Somehow, I managed to drag the dead soldier on board the plane while fighting continued to rage in the outskirts of the airport with the sound of gun fire and sound of explosions clearly audible.

I had to emulate my partner's method of carryimg the dead to be able to meet up with the order, in all I was able to count 77 causalities that morning, yet more continued to die.

At about 12 noon Major Ojo, appeared and ordered us to group ourselves into three equal batches. Within seconds, we were grouped into three different squad. A squad was assigned to consolidate our grip on the western part of the airport. Another squad was assigned to continue recoverng ECOMOG casualties and the third to escort the ECOMOG supplies to its headquarters. I found myself in the third squad.

The task turned out to be the most dangerous of the three assignments, it took about two and half hours to get all the supplies loaded on the Military trucks.

There were fifteen of the trucks and five personnel carriers that was briefly assembled and addressed by our commander. Major Ojo, who ordered "you must execute this assignments even if it means dying in the process," I jeered within myself, I was not going to die for another man's interest. I thought, and my thoughts drifted to Ajuma, wondering what she was up to at that moment.

Major Ojo, made his speech briefly and dismissed the muster parade for the assignments to commence, I foot-dragged so as to get on board the last personnel carrier and I succeeded with my intention. Within four minutes, our convoy of supply trucks and personnel carriers were already heading out of the Lungi Airport destined for ECOMOG's provisional headquarter in Freetown.

The convoy drove out of the airport using the eastern exit of the airport, but the fighting continued unabated on the Western exit. Sounds of machine gun firing relentlessly and exploding of hand grenade, mortar and rocket rounds could be heard clearly from our position as the convoy zoomed out of the airport.

We drove carefully and silently for about forty minutes without any incident. The smell of decomposing bodies filled the air as we drove on, the bodies of the war victims littered the streets. About 70% of the corpses I saw were of children and women, some lay stark naked, others have been badly burnt beyond recognition. All along I didn't see any living human on the streets.

I interrupted the silence when I was compelled to spit out, my body couldn't stomach the stench any longer. A soldier by my side laughed briefly and said, "You've not seen anything yet."

After a while, our convoy approached the only standing high structure on the street, at about 80km/p. Suddenly, a flash of light appeared ahead of us, accompanied by sounds of explosion which rented the air. The leading personnel carrier was almost hit by a mortar shell, all our attention were suddenly drawn to the explosion ahead of us which acted as a distraction from the rebels.

We immediately came under intense machine gun fire from behind. My Personnel carrier was worst hit been the last on the convoy. A powerful shot pierced through the skin of two soldiers sitting directly opposite me in the personnel carrier and their warm fresh blood gushed out of their skin spilling all over me. I quickly jumped out of the vehicle as it began to slow down, slowly rolling continuously before landing in a nearby ditch. I concealed myself where I had landed and immediately raising my rifle aiming at the direction of the machine gun fire.

By now pandemonium had griped the entire convoy. All the vehicles pulled over and all their occupants scrambled for a safe spot. While the machine gun continuously spraying its bullets in all directions.

From nowhere in particular, I heard orders blaring out to return fire. Shots rang out from our men in all directions toward the attackers, in response to the order. I fired several shots aimlessly toward the machine gun direction. I later seized fire and looked around me, I saw decomposed remains of three children lying around me. I was jolted by the sight and jumped out of the ditch like a frightened mouse.

I dashed toward a direction I was not sure of, somehow, I sighted another ditch and headed toward it but before I landed I felt a hot object hit my shoulder. As I landed, I saw my uniform stained with my own blood.

Someone shouted "Reuben are you alright," I refused to respond, severe pain enveloped me within seconds and I began to lose blood profusely. I immediately thought of Ajuma and wished again I had never joined the Army. The fire exchange continued and became more intense with each passing time. I summoned courage and raised my head and looked around, I saw the machine gun and it's bearer clearly, but was shaded by a small wall from the machine gun bearer.

I raised my rifle with the little strength that was left in me above my head and pushed the rapid button, and squeezed the trigger of my rifle pointing toward the machine gun position. My shot perforated the chest of the machine gun bearer and the gun became silent, the silence of the machine gun gave my colleagues the advantage to advance toward the machine gun position.

My blood continued to soak the ground around where I laid and my strength continued to reduce drastically, as the sound of machine guns and explosion rented the air, I then fell into a coma.

Faintly, I heard voices discussing. What I found difficult to understand was what time of the day it was, the discussion soon grew louder, then I heard someone call my name," Reuben Amana, how are you now," the voice kept repeating itself again, each time I tried to speak but couldn't "Reuben, are you alright", the voice called out again, "I am alright," I managed to answer.

I opened my eyes and I saw Major Ojo, standing beside my makeshift bed. I looked around the room with a blurred vision and saw a pint of blood hanging above my head.

"Sorry boy, you had a successful operation, you will be all right soon. See you later," major Ojo said, and he walked out of the room before I could say anything.

I had been evacuated after the fighting when I became unconscious and brought to the ECOMOG Medical facilities for treatment. I looked at the pint of blood hanging above my head and wondered if the blood had been screened for HIV/AIDS.

It took me twelve days to recover partially after which I was assigned to join the team of soldiers that provided security for the ECOMOG Headquarters.

Four days after my deployment, about forty ECOMOG soldiers were assembled, I was included and we were briefly addressed by the ECOMOG Field Commander, "soldiers, it has become a matter of great importance that we provide maximum security for the humanitarian workers in Sierra-Leone, considering the report I have just received that five aid workers were shot dead by the rebels yesterday, we have a big task ahead of us."

As the ECOMOG Field Commander explained, I felt blood rush up my face. Oh God, I thought, if I ever survive all this I will honour you forever, I saw no reason why we should risk our lives protecting people who meant evil for us.

The Field Commander said several things I failed to pay attention to, my mind drifted home, is Ajuma alright? Are my parents alright? How are they reacting to my deployment to fight for peace in another man's land?

After the address, the field commander walked away, and one lieutenant who called himself Yakubu took over the field commander's position and ordered us to split to four separate groups. The sound of explosions and gun fire could be heard from a far distance, while vultures littered the morning sky looking out for the war's fresh casualties.

"Hey you! Where do you belong?" Lieutenant Yakubu shouted, pointing at me "Sorry Sir," I murmured, immediately, as I sneaked into one of the groups waiting, "wetin you dey think mister man?" one of the soldier asked, and smiled at me. I ignored him and tried to look more confident than I actually felt.

Four white men wearing the Red Cross Emblem walked out of the ECOMOG administration Office and they stood beside Lieutenant Yakubu, He murmured a few words to them and the four of them walked forward joining each of the four groups of their choice.

"Hello gentlemen," the one who joined our group said "I am glad to have your company," he continued, "Corporal John, you will head your group. I have some humanitarian supplies you will distributed to civilians in Kabala," we remained attentive as he spoke about his mission and strategies to us. When he finished we all walked toward the waiting trucks, the sky was a mixture of smoke and vultures. I hung my rifle on my shoulder and jumped into the back of one of the waiting truck reluctantly and the other soldiers in my group joined me.

We drove in silence for about twenty minutes through the streets of Freetown with the white man directing the driver on which route to take. The truck finally pulled over front of a huge warehouse, and we were ordered out of the truck by Corporal John, who had sat beside the white man on the second roll.

Combat ready soldiers encircled the warehouse to prevent any attack or looting of the warehouse by intruders. Corporal John, escorted the white man into the warehouse and within minutes labourers started loading food, plastic containers, drugs and other supplies concealed in cartons into our truck, other trucks arrived the warehouse and formed a queue in front of its entrance waiting to be loaded.

The loading of our truck lasted for about thirty minutes, and Corporal John and the white man walked out of the warehouse, the white man held a sheet of paper in his hand and they both approached our truck. "Comrade," Corporal John, shouted, "it is important that this supply get to its destination in Kabala, two aid workers will join us on the trip and three of you will join in the distribution of the aid while the remaining will carry out guard duty," he paused briefly, then continued, "you, you and you," Corporal John, pointed to three of my colleagues, he, then said, "you will join in the distribution of aids while the rest of you must maintain security for the operation, got it," Corporal John asked, alright lets go."

We all climbed behind our respective truck with the two aid workers that had joined each truck. Three of my colleagues hung themselves strategically on the truck's body with their rifle fire-ready.

I sat inside the truck clinching to my rifle and thinking about what our fate would be when we arrived Kabala. After what seemed like a dramatic trip, we arrived peacefully and disembarked from the truck, at a place that seemed like an old burnt out market square. Within a few minutes, frightened and malnourished looking little children, woman and the elderly rushed out of their hideouts and surrounded the truck. I was assigned to safe guard the southern part of the market. I walked to my position quietly. I called on two girls of about 12 years old to help me lifted some old sand bag up to serve as cover for me. They gladly assisted me smiling each time. I felt very sorry for this little suffering children and wondering why they should suffered this terrible hardship they knew nothing about.

The distribution commenced peacefully but sounds of machine gun fire and explosion could be heard faintly from a long distance and smoke could be seen rising to the sky and smell of burning flesh could be perceived by anyone with a strong sense of smell.

''One after the other please, the supply will go round, be patient please,'' were some of the words I heard from my position blaring from a small megaphone the white man held to his mouth.

The supply had almost gone round everyone on the queue, everyone could be seen carrying something away to their hideouts, I watched quietly. Saying nothing. The two girls who had helped me erect a pillar of sand bags joined me after they had successfully carried their portions of the supply to their hideout

They both spoke a kind of Pidgin English I didn't quite understand but managed to make out some of what they were saying.

"Uncle! Where is your mother?" one of them asked, I was shocked by the question but somehow, I managed to find an answer for them, "my mother is in Nigeria," I answered, '' where is Nigeria?" The other asked. ''Nigeria is in Africa, do you know Africa?" I said, they both shrugged their shoulders, meaning they didn't know, I thought.

"Our mother is dead, she was cut with a knife by the RUF rebels, and they told my father to eat her flesh," one of the girls said. I was startled by what she said, "Where is your father?" I asked again "His hands was cut off with a knife by RUF, he died too." As I stood there listening, I could only watch these girls in horror and disbelieve.

God! Why all this? I exclaimed, how can humans be this cruel? "Who is caring for you two? I asked, "Nobody, just the two of us," one of them answered and pointed to a wall. "uncle," she called, I was carried away by the plight of this children I didn't notice a group of RUF rebels advancing towards me, she kept pointing at the wall and saying, "I see......," before she could finish the sentence, shots rang out from behind the wall and a bullet struck her on the chest knocking her flat on the ground.

Every one took to their heels amidst wailing and crying, I quickly pulled my grenade pin and threw the grenade at the wall, the grenade blasted the wall, the explosion gave me time to position my rifle and it stopped the advance of the rebels, before the dust of the explosion could settle I opened fire at the rebels' position.

The other girl was lucky, she fell to the base of the sand bag pillar in front of me. I kept discharging bullet at the rebels' position after fifteen minutes of intense gun battle, the rebels' fire eased.

"Reuben, withdraw, we must leave now," Corporal John ordered, "Rubbish you want us to leave the poor civilians alone? No way," I replied, not looking at his direction. Corporal John was silent, while the sound of more gun fire filled the air, I fired more rounds. From my position. It was quite easy to hit the rebels' line, so I kept reducing the numbers of the rebels' one after the other.

Corporal John had ordered the rest soldiers to get ready to withdraw. So, one after the other, they kept withdrawing to where the truck had been moved to for safety. In no time I was alone with the rebels when the rebels fired their shots at my position I returned fire with less intensity, my support had been withdrawn without my knowledge? I overheard the trucks engine roaring to life. By now the rebels had realized I was alone and were trying to take advantage of the situation.

"Girl! Girl!!" I called the little girl, "get ready to run to the truck, When I say run, run, do you understand," I yelled at the girl, "Yes Sir, I will run," she replied. I quickly changed my magazine, and shouted "run!" as I sprayed my bullets at the advancing rebels.

The girls ran like a cat in contest with a rat for safety, now she was safe, I had to withdraw. I seized fire and listened to the truck's engine, and it kept humming from the distance. Something gave me the courage to squat and run without shooting and I felt the strength of the rebels had been reduced because as I withdrew, I heard no gun shots anymore.

I safely reached a spot that provided another good cover for me, so I concealed myself there, "for the last time, Reuben, withdraw at once or you will be left alone here," Corporal John shouted. "this battle is won, and you are leaving the glory of victory behind. We must disperse these attackers John," I answered.

Two of my colleagues sneaked to join me behind the cover. If only Corporal John had heard the plights of those girls and watched one of them killed by the rebels he would have staked his life to wipe out the rebels completely. "Reuben, you are taking too much risk," one of my colleagues said, "shut up and fight those heartless rebels," I barked back at the two soldiers.

They both kept quiet and sneaked to separate safe covers, and shots rang out again from the rebel lines this time with less intensity, we responded with more aggression, when I saw that the rebels had little resistance to offer. I started advancing toward the rebels' position, my advance was aided by my colleagues, who fired to give me cover, and soon I reached a talking distance to the rebel lines.

"Lay down your weapons and your hands up or you all perish," I shouted in anger. While taking a good cover. Soon the rebels that were left obeyed my order to every one's surprise, they all came out of hiding with their hands up on a single file. I peeped and saw a boy of about fourteen years old among the RUF attackers. I became confused and asked," hey, three of you, are you a combatant or a captive? They didn't answer my question, they turned left and walked straight, "move" I ordered.

I ordered them to the open, and into our area of control, the other soldiers seized and tied them with electric cable from the wreckage of a building nearby. The air remained still and quiet, everywhere remained deserted. I walked to the rebel line, there I saw bullet ridden bodies of the rebels, mostly very young boys, I bowed in tears, why this senseless destruction, I asked myself, for the first time I saw it all unfold before my own eyes, 'child soldiers'. I carefully collected weapons of the rebels and took them on board our truck after dislodging the weapons. In all I counted twenty two dead bodies of the rebels, only two of our men sustained bullet wounds but they could get around without assistance.

My bravery at Kabala landed me in a big punishment, I was charged for insubordination, and was locked up by my Commander forty eight hours at the ECOMOG head-quarter, after my release, I was posted to guard some ECOMOG vital facilities around its strong hold in Freetown.

Each time my mind flash back to those two little lovely girls and how the other one was knocked dead by the RUF's bullets, it bothered me constantly.

After eight days of straight duty, I finally got two days break, the idea of writing Ajuma, came to my mind and I used the early hours of my first day off-duty to write my heart-out to Ajuma and I also wrote my parents, urging them to fast and pray for my survival but I was very careful not to tell them about my near death experiences. I knew their worries will increase if I tell them the truth, I dispatched the letters according to the laid down rules.

I thought I should take a walk around the safe part of Freetown to acquaint myself with the terrain and environment and also other things I need to know around here that may be of help to me later.

Dressed in mufti, I paired with Sule, a fellow solider. All long I have observed Sule to be a level headed soldier, and the most cultured of all my colleagues.

I stuffed a pistol into my hip-pocket, before we left our base, it was one I had recovered from a ten years old boy during one of our raids.

The streets of Freetown had nothing spectacular but debris of explosion-shattered buildings and decomposing corps littered everywhere, where are we going" I asked Sule, "Anywhere, you are more familiar with Freetown's streets. You should lead the way," Sule replied, the smell of decomposing bodies no longer irritated me. Pungent smell filled one street, we quickly walked through the street in less than half an hour by this time, we have strayed far away from our base into the distant streets.

We got to a street where little boys playing were football, when they saw us approaching, they paused, and watched us suspiciously.

I quickly said, "Who is the best dribbler here," the boys looked frightened at first but my question eased the tension a bit.

"I am the best dribbler," one of the boys answered. "Reuben! You join that team and I will join this team," Sule said, and he started rolling up his trouser, I did the same, and joined the other team "Alright let's go" I said, we played for about two hours.

Sweating and painting, my mind drifted away from the chaos around us, I have no doubt Sule enjoyed the game with the kids.

"Let's call it a day," Sule, I said, as I kicked the ball wild. "We've won, you are afraid," one of the boy said, "don't mind him they are afraid," Sule said in support of the boy. The boys in my team insisted we continue to play, but I was too tired to continue. Somehow, I convinced them to stop the game.

I promise we will be back tomorrow for a rematch, I reassured the boys as I rolled down my trousers and dusted myself of some dusty stains. "Reuben, look, our men on patrol," Sule said, I quickly looked around and saw the military personnel carrier with soldiers hanging strategically on its body.

We ignored the patrol team and only waved our hands in their direction, from the distance I recognized a couple of the soldiers.

We started our walk back to our base with optimism, together we trekked through the deserted corpse littered streets trying to find the right path and familiarizing ourselves with the streets. After half an hour walk, we got deeper into the outskirts of Freetown unknowingly, our optimism soon faded away into skepticism "are you sure we are getting closer to our base or further away?" Sule asked in desperation, "Don't worry, we will find our way," I said reassuring him.

The once busy street I thought has been turned into a ghost town, flies, maggots, dogs and vulture are the only living creatures that roam the streets majestically, the once beautiful structure has now been turned into a hip of rubble.

As we strolled silently, we approached a bend, and suddenly we were startled by a cat that dashed passed us as if it had been running an Olympic 100 meter race. We both paused abruptly.

"I missed that throw, that cat should call for a celebration tonight," was what we heard behind the bend. Sule, quickly jumped across a half blown out wall and took cover there, while I dashed under a burnt down vehicle by the side of the street and waited patiently amidst prayers that the intruders should be friends and not enemies. From my position Sule was completely invisible and I suddenly wished I had taken his position.

Moments later, a group of fifteen fully armed RUF rebels appeared from the bend, they stood at the street entrance studying the state of the street carefully. I froze when I saw them although the temperature was well above thirty three degrees that evening. My mouth dried up suddenly and I felt my heart beating faster than I could imagine.

They studied the street briefly but carefully, suddenly, I saw them advancing toward us, I touched my hip-pocket for my pistol and my hand came in contact with the pistol, I realized my pistol couldn't be a match for their automatic rifles and rocket launchers, how did those bastard murderers penetrate the ECOMOG line, I pondered quietly, not daring to breathe deeply, quietly, I crawled and rolled under a burnt out vehicle close to my hideout.

Any attempt to exhibit bravery here would spell doom for us, I thought. I watched the rebels with extreme fear, as they approached our hide out slowly. They were taking their time to look at spots where someone could take refuge. Some of the rebels probed holes and drains with cutlasses and sharp rod.

In no time the rebels were only six yards away from where I was, I felt like my live was melting to the ground where i laid, and my heart beat sounded like Sango's drum. My mind quickly made a fast judgement. I grabbed the propeller shaft of the vehicle I laid under and lifted my whole body completely off the ground and carefully hanged my weight on the steel pole of the propeller shaft, seconds after my entire body was fully concealed within the belly of the rusty vehicle, one of the rebel said something in their local dialect and he thrust a sharp iron rod under the vehicle, the rod scratched the hard tarred surface missing my body, by now I had stop breathing, even prayers seized to come to my mind. The rod scrubbed the ground several times, the sounds of the iron rod echoed repeatedly inside my head, but I remained motionless.

''Step back, this vehicle could harbour a threat'' one of the rebel said, no part of my body touched the ground, neither was I touched by the rod. But suddenly, I heard the cracking sound of a rifle intending to spray bullet on the rusty vehicle just then I heard a shout.

''I have one intruder here, come, quick, '' one of the RUF rebel shouted, the voice of Sule immediately cried out for mercy. "No! No!! I am a good friend," I heard footsteps run toward where Sule had concealed himself ''Shut up, you are a traitor and an intruder to Sierra-Leone," One of the rebel barked, ''good!! Where are your friends,'' another demanded, "I am alone, I have no friends," Sule answered in the most shaky frightened voice I have ever heard.

"Give him his right, a VIP treatment," a voice ordered "which do you prefer, long or short sleeve?" another voice asked. "Please, no, I have seven children in Nigeria. My mother is sick!" I heard Sule lament, "so you are a Nigerian, good,"

"Cut off his hand," a voice ordered, seconds later, I heard Sule's agonizing wails filled the air, "God! Sule's hand amputated, I thought, tears began to roll out of my eyes, as Sule's cry grew louder and more pathetic.

My grip tighten on the steel bar that hanged my body, "this man cries too much, lets finish him before he get us into problem," another voice urged, "No his superiors must see him alive like this," a voice said "Let's go!" Another ordered, three shots were then fired toward my direction, but none of the shot hit me.

The rebels matched on. But I remained under the rusty vehicle about twelve minutes after the rebels had vacated the scene, the cry of Sule had grown faint with each passing time, I was later able to put up courage and crawled out of the belly of the rusty vehicle.

With tears rolling down my cheeks, I ran to where Sule was laid motionless, I met Sule in his own pool of blood with both of his hands chopped off, down from his shoulder. I couldn't believe what I saw, the once handsome Sule now armless, "no, no, no," I shouted without realizing the rebels could still be around. I didn't know what to tell Sule, Would I have said sorry, or what, there I made up my mind to do the worst to those so called Revolutionary United Front rebels," Sule! Sule!!" I called out gently, "you will be all right," I said, in an effort to give him courage to survive this hell of a situation. Sule had lost so much of his blood, I tapered him gently on his back, "Reuben, is that you!" Sule murmured, amidst groaning, "yes, yes this Reuben you will be alright, am here," I replied in tears, the sun was gradually giving way to a dark cloud, I removed what was left of the sleeve of his shirt from his chopped off limbs with very shaky hands, and tied what was left of his hands to prevent further loss of blood.

I sat him down and allowed him to rest for about five minute; he kept groaning and was looking unconscious, I suddenly realize I had to take him to a health facility fast. Sule! "Please don't sleep here, Let's go back to base, please stand up," I said, as I helped him to his feet, with my right hand wrapped around his waist, I dragged him along, his bleeding was subsiding gradually but his blood still trailed us as we walked on.

The streets remained deserted and fear of any sort vanished from my mind, the task of saving Sule's life occupied every corner of my mind, I staggered alongside Sule, as we headed through uncertain routes, after about twenty five minutes trekking, Sule suddenly collapsed, I allowed him to rest for about three minutes, then I tried to revive him.

''Sule!!! We must move on please, get up, come on,'' I pleaded without success, Sule laid down motionless not moving any part of his body with his eyes close, I studied his amputated arms, his blood was beginning to cake on the amputated surface.

I tried every known tricks to revive Sule, but he had lost so much blood and his blood pressure had gone dangerously too low, I grabbed his trunk and dragged him off the street to a dark corner, I rested his back against a wall, I kneelt beside him, and I looked into his eyes closely, non-blinked I became more worried, if Sule will survive, I can't keep looking into his eyes like this, I thought and for the first time in hours, I started praying for him to survive. I prayed for about five minutes, suddenly, a burst of machine gun fire from a distance paused my prayer. I quietly crawled away from Sule, across the street I spotted an empty barrel laying on its side, I dashed across the street and pick up the barrel with both of my hand and lifted it over my head and ran back to where Sule was, I laid the barrel in front of Sule to act as cover for him, and I made a sign on his position for easy identification when I come back for him.

By now darkness had covered everywhere, using the darkness as cover and keeping to the sides of the shattered walls, I approach the direction of the gun battle. I felt the Rebels and ECOMOG troops must be the ones doing battle. I was not sure of the battle spot but carefully I advanced toward the battle area.

I soon came within a viewing distance from the battle spot, I realized I had to be extra cautious, so I paused and studied the area, it soon became clear to me that I was behind the rebel line, the rebels numbering about fifty had ran into a small patrol unit of ECOMOG soldiers, I made a proper assessment of the two different battle lines, and I soon realized that the rebels were in a better position to win the fight, as the gun battle raged on, my mind raced back to Sule, "God why all this," I thought, with a pistol I knew I was as good as harmless.

As my mind became preoccupied with the next step to take, I remembered I saw something like a multiple grenade launcher close to where I had picked up the barrel I used in shielding Sule. Without a second thought, I ran back to where I had picked up the barrel. I was less careful now, as I raced through the street. Luckily, I arrived there without any incident, and went straight to see how Sule was doing. I was surprised that Sule was gone, he was no longer where I had concealed him, "Sule! Sule!! It me," I whispered, desperately. I became confused as the blood stained floor couldn't give me any clue as to where Sule had gone. Should I go on looking for Sule or go for the rescue of my colleagues who were in danger zone, as this raced across my mind, a loud explosion from the distance jolted me back to reality.

I dashed to where I had picked up the barrel and I found a grenade launcher covered in dust and four live grenade cans lay inside a small gully nearby. Very quickly, I picked up the objects and ran towards the battle ground as fast as I could, neglecting to a large extent any precautionary measures.

Luckily, the rebels were not retreating, instead they were advancing on the ECOMOG's position, I carefully looked around for a good cover and I took position behind what I consider the best spot around, I had just four grenade but fifty rebels to hit and once I fire the first shot, I will no longer have a hiding place, it took me five good minutes to find my first most vital target which I must hit, fierce gun battle continued to rage and ECOMOG troops continue to lose ground to the rebels, the rebels were well spread along their line making the situation very difficult for me, but the target I spotted was a big plus for me.

Four huge black jerry cans stood close to a large ground of rebels, as it is the custom of the rebels to set buildings and their targets ablaze, so, I was sure the content of the jerry cans were petrol.

I carefully used four minutes to perfect my aim at the jerry cans. As I fired the grenade launcher there was a click and the grenade didn't fire, fear gripped me suddenly. I tried again, yet no responds from the launcher. I quickly abandoned the launcher and took three of the grenade and crawled towards the rebels carefully, I crawled through a drain where I occasionally stumbled on stinking decomposing human remains. I soon got close to the rebels and without wasting time, I pulled the pin of one of the grenade and threw it at the jerry cans, the grenade landed on target but refused to explode, The RUF rebels looked at the direction where the grenade land, "look," one of the rebel yelled, pointing a machine gun at my direction, that moment my mind told me its finish, but just that moment, the grenade exploded,

Everything went up in flames and more explosion was triggered off soon afterward. I was blinded for some seconds by the intensity of the blast and for some few moment the guns went silent on both side; the blast had come as a big surprise, to everyone, I quickly changed my hiding spot and waited in a ditch where i had crawled. Soon the gun fire resumed again, I pulled the pin of another grenade and toss it toward the rebels' position, and immediately an explosion blasted flame across the rebels' line. I kept myself concealed in my hideout. After about twenty two minutes of fierce gun battle, silence gradually crept behind both lines. "We surrender, we surrender," a voice cried behind the rebel line. A huge casualty had been inflicted on the rebels by my grenade attack. I heard instruction been handed out to the captured rebels far behind the ECOMOG line. When I was sure all the rebels had been securely apprehended, I shouted my units code name and my name three times as loud as I could, "come out," a voice urged me from among the ECOMOG troops. Carefully I stepped out of my hide out, still holding one live grenade.

Smell of burning flesh filled the air, carcases of rebels littered the surrounding area. Some terribly wounded rebels lay on the ground groaning in severe pain. A brief smile came across my face, and I was happy about the sight. If these animals could cut off Sule's hands, then, they deserve no pity.

Slowly, I walked toward the ECOMOG position and I went straight to a Lieutenant among the soldiers wearing an ECOMOG emblem and I introduced myself. "Sir, I am Private Reuben," the Lieutenant interrupted, "did you get behind the Rebel line my friend?"

"the Rebels attacked me and my colleague and they cut off his hands, when I heard the sound of gun fire from a distance, I came to assist you," I explained, "where is your friend," the Lieutenant asked, "He is missing now," I answered, " a soldier?" he asked, "yes Sir, he served in my unit," I said impatiently. "I have to search for him immediately, he was badly injured, both of his lands had been chopped off by the rebels," I explained in a calm voice,

"If his hands has been chopped off then, he is a waste now, I can't afford to commit any of my men to search for a burden," the Lieut. Said, "sir are you calling my friend a burden? It's unfair and inhumane, I don't need any assistance from any one, I will handle the situation alone Sir," I said.

I angrily walked away towards where I had left Sule, the Lieut., yelled out at me, "stop right there Reuben, I say stop," I ignored him and kept on walking. He didn't make any further attempt to stop me. I paused and picked up a machine gun abandoned by the Rebels, I checked the gun to see if it was still in order. The machine gun is an Israeli built sophisticated machine gun. When I was convinced that the ammunition were in order, I threw my pistol away.

I soon arrived where I had left Sule, there was still no sign of him there, and I became more worried. Carefully, I started tracing the blood stain on the ground, the blood stain led me for about three minutes and vanished, but I became more determined to find Sule at all cost. I raised my wrist to see what the time was but my watch was no longer on my wrist. I had lost it. I became even more upset, I roamed the streets around where Sule had disappeared for what seemed like three hours, and ignoring the dangers I was exposing myself to.

I spotted a dark corridor and approached the place carefully with my machine gun positioned ahead of me. I got to the corridor and saw nothing extraordinary. Concealing myself behind a short solid cupboard in the corridor, I waited to rest my aching feet. Silence engulfed the surrounding but for occasional long distant sounds of exposition and gun fires that punctuated the silence. The five minutes anticipated rest had stretched over twenty minutes now and I became reluctant about leaving my hide-out, and soon I fell asleep.

A "mew," sound startled me from my sleep, so I have been asleep, I thought. I felt very upset by my action, I immediately struggled up to my feet and picked up the machine gun, I was sure Sule could not have gone too far, as I took a step toward the exit of the corridor, I hard female voice from behind the building. I paused and listened very carefully, the voices kept on for minutes, very carefully I traced the voices to a dishevelled bungalow about 40 meters from my initial position.

Darkness enveloped the sky and the distance crow of a cock mixed with sporadic sounds of gun fire remain audible, as I approached the bungalow that seemed like a heap of wreckage from a recent hurricane incident, the voice kept whispering even as I became very close to the source. I still couldn't understand a word from the discussion, after a heap of trash I spotted a narrow passage, tiptoed through the passage holding my machine gun tightly, at the end of the corridor I saw a dilapidated cardboard shielding a narrow exit, there was no way to go through the exit without carrying the cupboard out of the way, lifting the cupboard out of the way will disturb the sleep of a tuatara. I thought. I decided to wait until someone attempts to pass through the exit.

I waited patiently and hoped that I should be able to find Sule alive, I waited for several hours and was determined to see if those voices am hearing could help me find Sule.

When day light was becoming slightly visible, I saw the cupboard move slow, by now the discussions had briefly subsided.

I froze suddenly in silent and looked around briefly, then jumped behind a pile of broken plastic sheets in the narrow passage, the cupboard kept moving until the exit became unobstructed, a slim female figure appeared from the exit slowly. My grip on the machine gun eased suddenly and I remained calm and watched the female figure step out completely with an empty plastic bucket, and walked passed me slowly toward the main street, she was completely unaware of my presence, I tried to stop her but something held me back. I allowed her to walk pass me, storming the hide out will be unwise, I thought. So I decide to wait for her and use her as a shield to break in.

After about two minutes she re-emerged and was walking faster now and carrying the bucket on her head as she took a step pass my hide out, I stepped behind her and gripped her from behind with one hand and my machine gun steady in my right hand. My action sent a deadly shock down her spine, she attempted to scream but my left hand quickly moved up and sealed up her mouth, I quickly whispered, "Friend! Friend!! ECOMOG," but before she could calm down her bucked slipped and the entire water spilled on both of us. After a few seconds she calmed down within my hard grip, and I suddenly felt how soft and enticing her body was. My mind then raced to Ajuma. I eased my grip slowly and allowed her move away slightly from me, when we were some distance apart, I then saw how pretty she was, slim, dark, tall with a perfectly shaped face and breast.

Apology ran out of my mouth without control, sorry, I am sorry, but I griped my machine gun in a combat ready position but I didn't point the gun at her. "Who is there with you?" I asked sharply, "my mother, who are you," she asked, "ECOMOG ……. And who?" I asked. She kept quiet looking at me, "Okay… move," I ordered her motioning her to lead me into the hide-out, as she walked past the exit I heard a voice say something I didn't understand but the girl kept quiet, as I walked pass the exit I saw an older female amputee sitting on the floor opposite the entrance, the woman on sighting me quickly struggled to her feet looking frightened. Mama! ECOMOG, the girl said, that word eased the tension on the woman's face, I looked to my right and saw an object rap in rags on the floor of the congested small apartment. I moved closer to the object and probed the object open.

What I saw startled me, Sule laid on the floor concealed among the rags, my mouth hung open in astonishment, I immediately threw my machine gun to the floor and grabbed Sule and shacked him awake "Sule! Sule!! Are you alright?" I shouted. Sule was still groaning in pains, his amputated hands had been treated and bandaged,

I shook Sule harder, "Reuben is that you?" he moaned in pains, "Yes it's me, how are you feeling?" Before Sule could respond to my question, I felt a chill still bar touched my neck, I froze and carefully looked toward the object, I saw my machine gun pointing at my skull. "Stay away from him," the girl ordered me, she had picked up my gun when I had dropped it. "I say move away from him, fast," she barked at me again. "what do think you are doing are you crazy? This is my friend" I said as I moved slowly away from Sule, "fast and get out or I will shot you," she yelled, the girl ordered me out and her threat and cruel tone send chills down my spine, "out! Step outside," she ordered again.

I quietly stepped out of the apartment, I heard the amputee woman whisper something to her. She responded with a clinched tooth, I couldn't understand their dialect. She led me to the corridor and my heart kept pounding, against my rib cage violently, "Girl, please don't do anything stupid. I will take you to Nigeria, I promise, be careful, the gun is loaded," I pleaded angrily. She remained silent and held the gun with her shaky hands.

When she was completely out of the apartment and in the corridor, she ordered me to stop. "You think you can trick me man," She lamented? "No, no girl I am an Ecomog soldier we are here to help you, your country, believe me, suddenly, shots rang out in quick succession behind me, I quickly turned around and grabed the gun as fast as i posible. Luckily, I was not hit by any bullet, I was terrified, I had secured the machine gun in my right hand and the girl was caught within legs, and I sat on her waist looking into her eyes, tears started rolling down her face, she sobbed.

I slowly stood up and gently stretched my left hand to her, she hesitated then grabbed my hand and I pulled her up. "Why do you want to kill me?" I asked very calmly, she kept sobbing, not saying a word, "I am sorry, I apologized, I don't mean to hurt you, and thank you for taking care of my friend," I said.

"I never want to kill you, I just want you to go away," she said amidst sobs. "I will go but with my friend, he has to go with me," I replied, she looked at me thoughtfully and said "man, I never want to shoot you, you look like my brother," she said while still crying, "where is your brother now," I asked calmly, "he is dead," she said. I felt sorry for her as I listened, "is that your mother?" I asked, "Yes, the Rebels came here and they tried to force my brother to join them, when he refused, they raped me, fourteen of the rebels raped me, he tried to stop them, they cut him with machete and shot him," she explained amidst sobs, I walked up to her and pulled her to myself with my left hand while the other hand held on to my machine gun. I hugged her and whispered into her ear softly, "it's alright, you will be alright, I will take you to the Ecomog camp.

I helped unwrap Sule off the rags he was covered in and sat him against the wall. I sat beside him on the dirty floor, Sule was still in terrible pains. "Sule you will be alright. I will soon get you to see a doctor," I said, "will he give me my hands back?" Sule whispered, I was deeply touched by the word that came out of Sule's mouth, tears quickly gathered in side my eyes, "yes, yes Sule, I promise you will be alright," I reassured him.

We both came into the tiny apartment where her mother was laying, I asked, "girl, am sorry, what is your name?" I tried to be as polite as possible "Nancy and my mother is Mrs Abraham, she answered calmly. "hurry up Nancy lets go. My friend is losing strength," I helped her gather some few things into a big leather bag and ten minute later we were ready to go.

I succeeded in getting Sule, Nancy and her mother to the Ecomog camp with the assistance of an Ecomog patrol unit we ran into just about eight minutes after we commenced the journey to the camp.

Sule was sent to the emergency unit of Ecomog health facility where he was placed under intensive care. I arranged for Nancy and her mother to get a shelter within the Ecomog safe haven for the internally displaced people.

The next day on the parade ground, Major Ojo had doubled me. "I received a very serious report about you this idiot," he said pointing his pistol at me, "you contravened the order of a superior officer during combat operation thus endangering the lives of the officers and men around you. You would have suffered grievous punishment but you will pay during operation, you will single handily dig all the trenches needed by your unit whenever the need arises. I am done with you," he concluded.

That morning I was very tensed up by the frequent distant sounds of explosions and gun fire, we remained at ease on the parade ground ignoring the approaching dangers, Major Ojo continued after a brief pause, "and the Rebel are pushing our men backward to wards Freetown you can hear the gun battle yourself, this unit will immediately be deployed to reinforce the retreating Ecomog troops," Major Ojo stressed.

Within minutes after Major Ojo's speech my unit was on board the military trucks that had been on standby. The truck I was in led the other trucks toward the front line. I prayed silently for my safety, knowing fully well that casualties are inevitable, the truck travelled slowly but steadily and each moment the distance sound of explosions and shooting steadily became more audible.

I stared lustfully into the sky as the trip dragged on, the image of Ajuma preparing, my meal flashed across my mind but occasionally punctuated by Nancy's smiling face. The fear of running over an anti-personnel land mine loomed in my minds. After about an hour twenty minutes drive, the truck came to a halt and other trucks followed suit. I suddenly became curious, we were all ordered to disembark from the trucks and to take cover.

"Hey Ajuwaya! Ajuwaya!!" The driver of our truck wailed. Captain UWEM who was in charge of our unit stepped out of his truck gorgeously, and ordered "come out every body, no cause for alarm," and we all stepped out of our hide-outs, I wondered who made Capt. UWEM, a captain in the army, he lacked every qualities of a combat unit commander. "Reuben! Come here, go and fill up that trench," Capt. Uwem said in Akwa-Ibom accent, while pointing to a deep trench excavated a cross the main highway by the rebels to slow down any reinforcement or retreat by peace keeping force. Quietly, I hanged my rifle on my shoulder and climbed into a truck and collected a spade. It took about twenty six minute to refill the trench while my colleagues stood by watching.

Sweat dripped off my body as I climbed back into the truck, "oh boy why not reserve his your sweat for the thirsty days, you are wasting water man," the soldier sitting next to me said, laughing, others joined in making jest of me.

We drove for just ten minutes and another trench forced our convoy to a halt, I was ordered to fill another trench, after about fifteen minutes' drive, we came cross another trench. In all I refilled six trenches within forty minutes.

Our convoy was about five kilometres from the scene of battle and the events on the battle front were becoming more vivid, smoke raising to the sky and heavy artillery round pounding the distance land scape relentlessly mixing with choruses of machine guns fire.

The last trench we came across appeared deeper than the other trenches I had encountered earlier, worse still more trenches scattered around the dusty road making it more difficult to refill. I struggled for about twenty minutes to partially refill the trench somehow without any assistance, my entire strength seemed drained, and I decided to collapse inside one of the partly covered trench.

Two of my colleague rushed out and dragged me up to my feet, I was taken to the side of one of the truck and I rested against one of the trucks wheel, and I was left there to sweat profusely. Five minutes later I was helped by one of my colleagues onto a truck and soon we commenced the trip.

The weight of my rifle now seemed like the weight of an Iroko tree. I allowed my rifle to rest on my thigh, and we drove in silence until we arrived at the battle front. Our convoy was flagged down by fleeing Ecomog soldiers.

The trucks pulled off the main road into a nearby bush. "Every one out of the truck and assemble for posting," Capt Uwem ordered, A few minutes into the address, a shell landed some few meters away from where we assembled, every one raced for cover, from where I laid on the ground I could hear the Captain. Wailing amidst the cracks of gunfire and explosion issuing impracticable orders like, "advance from the right flank, climb the tree for better position," while he buried his head behind a huge tree truck for cover. I wished the ground could open up for me to bury myself.

I stretch my rifle forward and I released the safety catch, I fired several shots aimlessly into the distance shrubs, soon Capt. Uwen's impracticable orders eased up and I heard the roaring of a trucks hurriedly retreating from the rebel advance we would have withdrawn back ward, the rebels were already pushing us fiercely backward.

Gun shots kept firing sporadically, when I looked at Capt. Uwen's position again, he had disappeared, I looked curiously around and saw nothing but smoke and dust, I then called out "Captain! Captain!!"

The captain was not insight, but in a short while I saw the Captain dashing toward the retreating trucks. God this man is running away, I thought.

I felt like turning my rifle on him but something restrained me, how could he abandon us here, I crawled and fired several shots aimlessly toward the advancing RUF rebels, somehow the huge mortar gun attached to one of the trucks was wheeled into the bush and strategically positioned.

When the first shot zoomed out of the barrel of the gun, it flew over my head, and i quickly retreated behind the gun, the gun kept discharging mortal rounds at the rebel positions. Other multiple grenade launchers supported the mortar gun raining explosives on the rebel line. This intense bombardment slowed the rebel advances greatly.

Explosives from the rebels also pounded our position, forcing some of our men to retreat further backward leaving us in the middle with the mortar and the three grenade launchers. We kept pounding each other's line with bullets and shrapnels, but the impact of our rounds had more devastating toll on the RUF rebels' side.

Each time I discharged some shot into the space in front of me, I hope that somehow my shot will pierce the skull of a one those poorly kitted ragtag rebel, they kept coming at us. The battle raged on for hours. The heavy mortar fire and the multiple grenade launcher succeeded in halting the further encroachment of the rebels on our frontline. But each time the fire is directed at the rebels, our ammunition kept reducing with little or no replacement at all.

I kept praying that the rebels should be on their heels before we fire our last round of mortar shell, the reduction in the fire power of the rebels boosted the morale of our men and some crawled to join our position afterward.

I laid on the ground, and it helped me to rest from my previous exhaustion. The artillery exchange raged on while our battle line continued to be reinforced by our men who had earlier retreated.

Just as we were contemplating to push forward, a helicopter gunship roared to sight from behind the enemy line. The fire power of the helicopter was so enormous that our mortar was silenced by the helicopter for a while. From the time the helicopter came to sight, almost all our shot were targeted into the sky in an effort to hit the helicopter, but the helicopter had a way of escaping our shots. As the battle raged on, the rebels were gradually gaining the upper hand again because of the deadly support the helicopter gunship provided.

Some of our men withdrew, while, others were hit during their attempt to flee backward, I remained entrenched in my hide out while shooting at blank targets. Occasionally, the rebels in the distance tried to switch position. The helicopter terrorized us for about thirty minutes before disappearing, probably to refuel.

The battle raged on with none of the two frontlines gaining anymore my ground. Later, I noticed I was beginning to run shot of ammunition, so I cleverly reduced the frequency at which I fired but soon I saw some soldier bringing in fresh mortar rounds to our artillery position this development gave me some leap of hope that the artillery pounding of the rebels will be sustained. The fear of the helicopter re-emerging kept our plan to advance silent, the sun had started its retreat to the east, and I imagined how I could pass the night half buried in a trench.

As the night approached the fighting gradually became less intense. The sound of trucks approaching and leaving the theatre of war occasionally interrupted the prevalent sound of gun fire and explosions. The wounded and the dead were carefully taken away in those trucks.

An order was issued that on no account should we retreat, that arrangements were on to get in more reinforcement. This directive came to us via a megaphone. The night soon enveloped everywhere and the sound of insects like crickets and even frogs came alive,

The fighting had greatly eased. The night dragged on very slowly with no end in sight to the hostilities. My mind soon started darting from one imagination to the other as we laid for hours.

When it became apparent that fighting had eased, I sat up and rested my back against a nearby tree trunk, waiting for nature to roll up the darkness. The cover the darkness provided was used to distribute suppliers ranging from ammunition, food and water.

As I ate my meal quietly, I thought of how this could be a peace keeping mission, when the Sierra Leoneans we are here to help and their jobless friends from other neighbouring countries kept killing us, the so called Peace Keepers, and we in turn kept hunting them like games.

I carefully reloaded my rifle and munched my meal quietly. Half way into my meal, shots rang out behind me, I quickly took cover and stirred my rifle toward the direction of the gunshot, '' RUF rebel, I saw a rebel cross that place," I had a voice lamenting in the dark, not too far away from my position, I stared out motionlessly, looking into the dense darkness for any false move or sign of life but I saw nothing. Then something stung me, neglecting all caution, I jumped up and grabbed the spot. I looked at the spot in severe pain but the darkness blind folded me, I almost cried out in pain but I quietly held onto my ground. Another sting close to my armpit made me jump even higher, I hastily removed my shirt and underwear, dusting it carefully.

Then another shot echoed from the distance, I plunged into the grass again for cover while I groped blindly for my rifle, and without a return shots fired. Silence once again engulfed the area, and I went on my knee and carefully dusted my shirt before putting them back on. The pain from the poison the insect injected into my skin gave me serious thoughts. Could it be a scorpion or a snake, I thought, because I didn't see what actually stung me, it aggravated my worries and the night was far from over.

I remained on my knee groaning silently. Occasionally, shots were fired from both end of the frontlines. But no one dared any tricky advance, I listened to the sound of local insects in absolute darkness and I wished I was one of the insects. The insects had nothing to worry about, they're just living their lives I thought. They seemed to be completely ignorant of the deadly situation we've been dragged into by our political leaders, but the insects don't do politics, they just live. The night dragged on very slowly while I nursed my insect bite quietly with prayers that the pain should vanished and somehow it miraculously eased.

The night kept going, soon the distance crow of a cock came to us, it signified that we were approaching day break. At about five thirty in the morning, gun fire erupted but I refused to fire any shot because I didn't see any target and I didn't want to give up my position, but I maintained a very high level of readiness, shoots kept hammering out and after a while it seized. "They must go back, they must go back," a voice kept shouting from the distance and the voice later faded away.

By day light I saw where my remaining food had landed on the ground after the insect sting. Reinforcement arrived that morning and carefully they were dispatched to various spots along our line, moments after the deployment was completed, the helicopter roared into the air and started attacking our frontline.

The mortar and grenade launcher immediately resumed its bombardment of the rebels' position. A portable surface to air missile launcher had been brought in during the early hours of supply. When the occupants of the helicopter noticed that missile had been fired at them, they started to use heavy calibre gun to fire at our positions. How could the RUF rebels afford an air support while a regional peace keeping force could not, it baffled me. It's obvious they were getting support from a third country. It then dawned on me that we were fighting a proxy war.

The helicopter pounded our position with explosives for about thirty minutes before a shot from a surface to air missile launcher struck the helicopter, forcing the helicopter to make a hasty landing. With the helicopter out of the way, the strength of the rebels was greatly diminished.

The artillery kept pounding both lines. I kept as close to the ground as possible, shooting only when a target was on sight. That way, I was able to greatly reduce shooting fatigue. When it was becoming clear that the rebels fire power were diminishing, some of our men starter a slow but steady advance toward the rebel lines. I remained entrenched to my position, soon I heard, "Move!!! Advance," the orders forced me out of my safe hide-out into the bullet and explosive infested bush.

As I crawled forward I tried never to be too smart, the advance was very slow but steady, the shelling continued with shells landing occasionally on some of our entrenched men. And by noon, we had succeeded in pushing the rebels backward into the countryside, and once more the main highway leading to Freetown was under ECOMOG control.

I remained on the frontline for four days that seemed like four years. Although, there was no further outbreak of fierce fighting during my attachment to the front, but at night occasionally skirmishes do occur between ECOMOG and the RUF rebels who tried to infiltrate the Ecomog area.

I was later withdrawn. The trip back to base was quit boring but somehow the truck arrived ECOMOG base safely without incident. I immediately went straight to the health facility where Sule had been under intensive care. I arrived there feeling sticky and smelly as I have not had any bath for several days.

A military nurse, approached me at the entrance to Sule's ward. "Excuse me, is there any way I can help you?" the nurse said politely. "Hmmm, Please, I am private Sule's friend, I want to see him," I had hardly finished speaking when a loud male cry engulfed the hall way, "yeeee!! my mama oh, God! God!! Save me," the voice wailed relentlessly, "what is going on there," I asked politely, "He was wounded in action, and his left leg had to be amputated, his injuries are terrible," the nurse replied, "my God, you mean you don't have the drug that will put the poor man to sleep?" I asked angrily, his cry continued, interrupting our conversation. "So, how is Sule," I interrupted, "Sule has been transferred to Lagos yesterday," the nurse replied, "you mean he is okay now," I asked impatiently, "No, I mean Sule didn't make it, he failed to survive despite our efforts," the nurse said calmly, I was frozen by a remark, I suddenly dropped my rifle on the floor, and the Nurse quickly stepped back in fear. "You mean Sule is dead," I asked again, the nurse didn't say anything and only stared at me. I quickly picked up my rifle and walked out of the Ecomog field clinic with tears streaming down my cheeks.

The last six months was quite traumatic for me. I somehow managed to execute my assignments. Sometimes below standard, my urge to quite the army grew stronger by the day, if all this close colleagues of mine could suffer such terrible fate, I felt mine was around the corner somewhere waiting to happen, my plans has always been centred around Ajuma, I could run back to Lagos and take

Ajuma to a safe place and together we could make the best out of our lives.

The last time we met, I had promised Nancy and her mum that I will come and spend my next duty free day with them. Since I met Nancy and her mum, they've considered me a perfect friend, lately, I and Nancy had been exchanging glances that has made me uncomfortable, but Ajuma's love kept burning deep down in my heart and it kept any funny act far away from my mind.

As I approached the Ecomog Safe Haven for the Internally Displaced Persons (IDP) camp to pass my work free day with Nancy, she sighted me from a distance and ran out and embraced me warmly. "Welcome, and thank you for keeping your promise," she said, while still holding my hand, she led me through what seemed like a sordid environment, to a small space where a blanket was laid on the ground, I Looked around and spotted her mother and greeted her warmly.

Carefully, I occupied a small but comfortable space on the blanket. "what do I offer you Reuben," Nancy asked, I parted my lips in a brief smile, "I should ask you that question, Nancy," I said, "so, how are you coping with your mother health condition?" I asked softly. "My Mummy and I are okay, you have helped us a lot, I must confess Reuben, I don't know how to thank you," Nancy explained.

Her Mum laid quietly and soon moved out of my sight. When I looked around the shed, I didn't see any sign of her, Nancy sat directly opposite me allowing me to have a perfect view of her excellent body, her wonderfully shaped lips parted occasionally in a smile when I said something that amused her. Nancy's beauty is no doubt charming to any normal man.

At times I prayed, and wished that Ajuma will appear before my eyes miraculously, gently I disclosed what had happened to Sule to Nancy, she yelled in shock, "But he was feeling better when I went to visit him, three days back, he told me lots of stories about Nigeria, which made me want to go to Nigeria, how come he now passed on?" She said in an emotional laden tone with tears rolling down her pretty cheeks. I don't know, I replied.

We remained silent for a while. "Can't you be happy for once?" I asked when tears kept dropping down her cheek. "I will be alright Reuben, promise you will stay with me," she said, "but I am here with you," I replied, I brought out a pack of cards and spread it on the floor in front of us. We played the cards together silently, occasionally looking into each other's eyes. Moments later, I urged Nancy to take a walk with me to a nearby market within the Camp.

"You refused to accept anything from me Reuben," Nancy said, as I squatted to arranged the cards, she stood right in front of me slowly, I will accept anything you offer me Nancy I answered. I stood up and shoved the cards into my hip-pocket. Alright let's go, she held on to my hand as we walked toward the market together. "This moment reminded me of my brother, he was such a nice guy. I miss him a lot," she said, "I hope I am helping you get over all this?" I asked her, "Yes, you have been so nice, I wish we are always together," Nancy said, There's this inexplicable urge that kept burning within me like wildfire.

We got to the market and bought some groceries. And we soon discovered that aids meant for the refuge population somehow found its way into the market and were been sold at ridiculous prices. We shopped for about thirty five minutes, sluggishly strolling through the market.

She carried the items alone and didn't allow me help her. I let her please herself and we soon got to the hut in no time. There was still no sign of her mother. I went straight to the blanket on the ground and laid on it while Nancy went to start preparing for the cooking. I soon dosed off. I slept for about three hours. When I woke up, I opened my eyes and saw Nancy fanning me, I couldn't believe it, I wiped my face several times with my hands, "how long have you being doing this?" I asked her and gently seized the hand fan from her. She didn't give me any answer but instead, walked out of the hut, she later came back with a steaming plate of meal. "You have to eat now Reuben" Nancy urged.

I drank out of a cup of water she kept beside the blanket, and washed my mouth outside the hut and returned to my previous spot on the blanket, "thank you for this sumptuous delicacy," I said grabbing one of the spoons placed beside the plate. I took several munches. "wow! This is delicious," I exclaimed. "Thank you," Nancy said. We ate together in silence. "Where is your mother?" I asked curiously. She has gone to see her childhood friend not too far away from here she answered.

After the meal, she cleared the dining spot and went to the back of the hut where I believe served as their kitchen. She later returned to join me on the blanket. We sat side by side and I brought out the card and started shuffling it. " Reuben, tell me about your mother," Nancy asked looking straight into my eyes. "I don't know where to start, Nancy, you have to ask me specific questions about her and I will give you the answers one at a time" I replied.

I quickly shuffled the cards and somehow maneuverer her mind to other topics that captivated her interest. "when do you hope to get married Nancy," I asked, "It depends on when I get a nice guy" she answered, she hesitated then continued, "some of your colleagues take advantage of Sierra-Leonean women, they use and dump them at will. "I agree with you, that is what some of those so called peace keepers do, lots of sierra Leonean women are now pregnant for these men who they don't really know, and who care less about them, she said.

I had a very nice time with Nancy that day, I made her open up her mind about several issues and she got my 0pinon on several important issues too. Then night had began to creep in gradually, when I stood up and stretched my body. "Nancy, I have to go back to my base," I said. "I thought you were going to stay much longer," she complained. "I will be back tomorrow," I pleaded, as she accompanied me hand in hand to a junction and after several hesitations, we parted.

Since I arrived Sierra Leone for this peace keeping mission about six months ago, I realize that Nancy had succeeded in playing a bit of Ajuma's role in my life, but deep down in my mind no woman can take the place of Ajuma in my heart.

I arrived my base soon after, and went straight to my bunk bed. "Reuben you have a letter," Ibrahim, one of my colleague said as he approached my bunk bed with a brown envelope, I was gripped by curiosity, and I couldn't wait to open the letter, when I finally did, it reads –

My Dear,

I hope you are alive and well? How is everything? Words cannot express how I have missed you dearly.

I have been trying to get in touch with you since you left me, but it has not been easy, I hope this letter get to you in good health and peace.

Since you left me, it's not been easy. I got the note you wrote but no one has ever given me a penny, I have approached everyone in charge of your battalion, but no one gave me the money you promised to send. I have been trying to survive doing petty trade but your brother is not helping matter either. I am very sorry to complain about him, but he is giving me lots of problem here.

I am alright, so are your parents and every one, I will always love you forever, be very careful in all you do, I pray for your safe return always, and you should not forsake prayers, pray always I am sure God will save you.

Yours only,
Ajuma.

I read the letter twice before looking around me to thank Ibrahim for delivering the missive, "Ibrahim," I shouted, but I got no response, I guessed he walked away while I was busy reading the letter. What is all this? I thought aloud. "Why have they refused to give my wife part of my salary as I had instructed?" I became very upset. My urge to quit the Army became even stronger. It was late so I couldn't log any complain to my supervisor officer. How could I starve my wife of the basic necessity of life because I want to be in the Army. And that night I wrote a reply to Ajuma's letter.

The night was long and boring, as I didn't sleep a wink. The thought of Ajuma been reduced to a mere barrack woman who does petty trade troubled my mind throughout the night. I hoped she realize I didn't intentionally starve her.

Very early the next morning, I hurried off to the commandant's office to make my grievances known, I still wore annoyance on my face as I walked into the office.

"Yes! What do you want?" One of the soldier attached to the commandant's office said, moving to block my access to the office. "I want to see the commandant now," I demanded angrily, "come back by 1pm," the soldier replied, his casual response made me more angry. I took a deep breath in an effort to ease my temper. "Okay, I will wait for him here," I said. "Why must you wait here?" he replied, "you are not allowed to wait here, it's an order," the soldier yelled.

I took a few steps backward and I felt like swinging a smacking punch at his fat oily face, but somehow I controlled my temper, I turned round and dashed out of the entrance of the office and I went straight under a tree shade close to the office and waited there.

Staring straight at the entrance of the office. I waited there until seconds became minutes and minutes soon elapsed and became hours. When the waiting became monotonous for me to endure. I stood up from the top of the stone I had been sitting on all along, the blood flow to my lower body had completely been hampered. So I stood up and stretched out in ought most disappointment.

While I waited, my eyes spotted a female figure dressed in a pink coloured silk long gown coming out of the entrance of the Commandant's office. I was perplexed, what is going on? I thought, as I squatted quickly to conceal myself. I saw the commandant emerged behind the lady as I looked on, then he made a few gestures and a jeep pulled up in front of the lady and whisked her away. The commandant then turned around entered his office. My mind darted round several things. I waited for a few minutes. I then stood up and walked towards the office, when I entered the office, I looked at the wall clock, and it was already 14:15hrs. I shook my head in disgust.

Another soldier approach me at the entrance. "Yes, any problem?" He asked, "I want to see the commandant," I demanded, he brought out a sheet of paper and pen from his breast pocket, "Take and fill this visitor's form," he ordered, I accepted the form and filled it with shaky hands, I then handed the form back to him "wait there, am coming," he ordered as he stepped into the Commandant's office.

Some few minutes later he emerged and ushered me in. he led me through a couple of corridors before pointing to a door.

I turned the door handle gentle and stepped into the large office. The office was very air conditioned and largely spacious office with polished mahogany furniture neatly arranged. Right behind the commandant's chair, I saw a mattress neatly folded. Sheets of paper doted his desk. I spotted the form I had earlier filled in front of him, I stood at attention and saluted Commander Ojo, "morning sir!" I said, "Yes, I am on my way out now, what do you want?" I swallowed a lump of sputum before clearing my throat, I explain what brought me to his office briefly. "is that all?" he snapped, cutting me short of words. "yes sir," I replied, "fill your particulars here," he said as he pointed to a piece of paper on his table.

I hurriedly wrote out my particulars on the paper. "attach your letter to the paper and give it to me," he ordered. I used the stapler on his desk to do the stapling, "ok you can go, I will forward your complain," he concluded, I came to attention briefly again to salute him and turned around and left his office. When I got to the exit of the building what I saw startled me, I met Nancy's sweaty lovely face waiting for me. I almost cursed but somehow I refrained. "What are you doing here," I asked in an unpleasant tone. She beamed her smile at me and said, "I waited for you but you didn't come, I was afraid," she said mildly "of what?" I cut in, she hesitated then said, "for you, please, don't go looking for me again," I cautioned, the smile on her face stiffened and disappeared, I felt sorry for been too hard on her. I quickly eased my tone to diffuse the tension I had created.

How is your Mum? I asked mildly holding her hand as we walked side by side. "she is fine," she replied, I managed to make her smile again after a few jokes, we later arrived her hut together hand in hand, she had prepared another meal which she brought out from a corner of the hut and placed it on the blanket. She told me she had not eaten since morning and had been waiting for me to show up. I listened in absolute confusion, my mind silently pondered over what she meant.

After the meal I straightened out on the blanket and my mind drifted to Nancy's Mum. "Sorry, where is your Mum?" I asked curiously, "she went to pass time with her friend down the street there," she replied while pointing her hand toward a direction beside the camp, I didn't say anything. I tried to relax, but she laid right beside me, thereby making it difficult for my mind to be at rest, despite the horrific situation she's being through, she remained very attractive, with succulent skin. I was tempted to touch her but I drifted to sleep.

I slept for hours, when I woke up I found her fast asleep beside me sweating with a hand-fan in her right hand. I guess she had been fanning me before sleep knocked her off. I gently picked up the fan and started fanning her, the hut was a bit hot and the breeze was still, my fanning soon dried her sweat and her beauty continued to tempt me as I stared at her, but in my mind I exercised restraint.

About thirty minute later, Nancy opened her eyes and saw me fanning her, she quickly sat up and embraced me and thanked me for fanning her, she sat upright and thanked me for caring, I wish the embrace could last a little longer but it didn't.

When it became too dark for us to distinguish the cards, I decided to park up, "Nancy. I think it's becoming dark, let's take a walk," I pleaded. We roamed the surrounding areas within the Ecomog protected zones hand in hand. I felt relief she was spending some moment of joy with me. Later that night, I accompanied her back to her hut, her mother had returned and I went in to greet her briefly.

She saw me off gain, "Nancy, please, I think you should go and stay with your Mum," I said, Mum is alright she replied, "I know, ok, I will accompany you back to the camp. Promise you will go and stay with her," I pleaded, "If that is what you want, I will go," she said, good girl, I said excitedly.

When we arrived Nancy's shelter, I was becoming a little stressed up and tired, "Nancy I will make sure I see you immediately after my next tour of duty, I said, "Reuben, please be careful, don't play James Bond for any reason, run when others do," she said in a pitiable tone. "careful Nancy, be careful too," I replied, and then I turned to leave. "you are forgetting something gentleman, "she said mildly, my mind suddenly reminded me that she wants a peck, I drew her closer and give her a nice quick peck, "thank you," she humbly said while staring straight into my eyes, "alright I will see you then," I said and after a brief moment of silently staring at each other thoughtfully, we parted.

I got to my bunk bed a little later than yesterday, most of my colleagues had gone to bed, knowing the hell of task ahead of them tomorrow, "oh boy, you are back," Ibrahim said from a dark corner I didn't expect to hear someone's voice, I turned abruptly toward his direction before responding, "a message from Nigeria, do you have an idea of what our duty will be like tomorrow?" I asked as I laid down on my back, "I heard the rebels are pushing fast toward Freetown and General Mosquitoes is claiming he will over run Freetown with his R.U.F Rebels," Those were the only words I remembered hearing before I drifted into a deep sleep.

We were all jolted to life by a blaring horn from a truck, the individual task of the previous day had knocked my entire unit into a deep sleep, and before I could roll my body out of my bed reluctantly, orders of an emergency deployment had started been served to us. I hurriedly dressed up for combat and in no time we all assembled, we were hastily briefed that we were going to repel the advance of the RUF rebels & the military Junta in Freetown from the mile 91 front. The address was one of the shortest ever as a result of the urgency of the operation.

With my rifle sticking out above my shoulder I climbed behind one of the five trucks that were at hand to convey us to the frontline, I took a left row seat, and hoped for good luck in our operation

Throughout the course of the trip I didn't speak to any one and I declined commenting on any raised issues, I only fondled my rifle all along.

The blast of heavy mortar announced to everyone that we've arrived the frontline. Every one hurriedly disembarked, I was paired with six other soldier to tame the rebels advance from a hilly terrain east of the frontline. Some Ecomog soldiers had kept other sections of the frontline busy and difficult for rebel activities, but my section of the frontline was void of any Ecomog position so the rebels had already made huge gain before our deployment. The frontline comprised a long stretch of hilly grassland with a narrow path in between.

The first two hundred meter push into the frontline was easy for us, thereafter, we were confronted by very stiff opposition from the rebels thereafter. Our rocket launcher bearer had to crawled ahead of us when it became obvious that the rebels were unleashing severe attach on us. I laid where my head was shielded by a piece of rock of about a foot wide, I kept shooting into the distance where my mind told me. It was impossible to see anyone but the glow of the nozzles of gun occasionally gave out some rebel position. I explored such break whenever possible to fire at definite targets.

After several minutes of intense shelling by Ecomog artillery unit, the rebels' resistance slipped, giving way for my unit's incursion on the rebel's position. When I was sure it was safe to abandon my shelter, I got to my feet, keeping as low as possible, I followed my other colleagues who were already in pursuit of the retreating rebels.

The echoing sounds of automatic gun fire made it impossible for any other sound to be heard, I kept to my right, trailing the rest of my colleagues few minutes after the chase began, I was amazed by the spate at which the rebels abandoned their line of defence, I became suspicious and extra careful not to stumble on a booby trap.

I heard the soldier who led our incursion shouting at the top of his voice. He was now very excited about the ease of this fight, I could hear him chant "Nzobu Nzobu Eyin Ba Eyin," a Nigerian dialect victory song.

The sudden blast of an explosion threw a brief blanket of silence over the frontline. I quickly threw myself to the ground in confusion. The song suddenly died out due to the sound of the explosion and the bright light that accompanied the blast gave me a view like a man in the midst of a fire. Before I could make out what was wrong another colleague of mine who was just a few meters away from where I landed, saw clearly how a fellow soldier was ripped apart by a mine. I was amazed that his legs were spared but his torso was blown open by the explosion.

I suddenly absorbed the fact that the RUF rebels had littered the front with anti-personal mines. Moment after the second blast, an uneasy calm enveloped the frontline.

Muni, Muni are you alright, a voice asked faintly, I slowly lifted my head from where I had buried it in fear and looked around me to see who the owner of the faint voice was. Then another voice called out again. ''Gomani!!!

I looked around gain to see the unfolding events, This time my eyes captured Gomani just a few meters away from me, ''Gomani are you alright,'' I asked, ''please call our Rev. captain to pray for me. I don't want to go to hell,'' Gomani replied faintly. ''Gomani, you will be alright,'' I said, ''I see hell this moment, God, please forgive me,'' He cried in agony.

Very consciously I lifted my rifle and crawled to where Gomani laid, careful enough not to disturb the soil, when I got there I found Gomani soaked in his own pool of blood, I knelt in front of him and turned him over, what I saw nearly knocked me unconscious, Gomani's chest and stomach had been ripped open by an anti-personnel land mine, he had stepped on a land mine mistakenly, each time he opened his mouth to speak blood gushed out of his mouth uncontrollably.

Call the Reverend, I want to pray, Gomani said faintly amidst gasp. I immediately saw him relaxed suddenly, the up and down movement of his chest came to an abrupt end, and he stopped breathing and just then private Muni crawled to my side shivering in terror.

''Reuben, is he alright,'' Muni asked, Muni sorry, he is badly hurt, I tried to explain, but a sudden outburst of gun fire made us dock for cover. I hurriedly crawled to the left side of the frontline, there I found a hiding place, and I quickly concealed myself behind the cover and returned fire with my automatic rifle. After several minutes of gun fire with the rebels who wanted to capitalize on our casualties, we received fresh deployment of Ecomog combatants. The distant bang of explosions and heavy machine gun fire made it clear to even a blind man that hostilities was far from over.

The fighting on the frontline grew intense daily due to the importance of the contested area to both the RUF and the government of Sierra Leone, reinforcement arrived at the frontline almost on daily bases. Both side of the conflict suffered very serious casualties, the rebel later withdrew their fighters due to the heavy price they paid in human lives and military hardware.

I was redeployed after the RUF withdrew from the frontline to another unit lead by a Ghanaian army Major Kweku Jerry. He took the stand and address the parade one morning, he was brief and exact in his approach, he said my unit will head toward Makeni the RUF stronghold and launch an attack meant to harass and destabilize the RUF's command and control apparatus.

Makeni is the fourth largest city and economic nerve centre of the Northern Province, Makeni is the capital of Bombali district, the city is about 137 kilometre east of Freetown in Sierra Leone, the city of Makeni is home to the University of Makeni which is the largest private university in Sierra Leone and also the St. Francis Secondary School, one of the most prominent secondary schools in the country.

"We are a multi-national force with the international community backing and our superiority must be felt by those out-lawed rebels," the Ghanaian said conclusively. As we filled into the waiting military trucks, "Reuben! The commandant wants to see you immediately," one of the commandant's aid said as I attempted to climb one of the truck. I was filled with curiosity as to what the matter was.

When I got to his office, the commandant was dressed in his full military combat gear and he sat majestically on his wooden armchair. "Morning Sir," I saluted as I stood at attention, "yes, who was the young lady that traced you to this place the day you came to complain," he asked, the question freaked me out, I hesitated, "the young lady, which young lady Sir?" I murmured in a depressed tone, "you are a vagabond, are you questioning me?" The Commandant said angrily. "No sir," I replied, "sorry sir, sorry Sir," I pleaded, then the horn of one of the truck blared sharply, "Alright, when you are back from duty, I want to see you and that girl here unfailingly," he ordered. I took a step forward and saluted him again, "so you know what is good?" he asked. And without responding I ran out of his office to board the last truck on queue.

During the trip to Makeni my mind drifted from one issue to another. What on earth does this Ghanaian commandant want with Nancy, I thought. But my mind refused to believe my imagination. I made up my mind to protect Nancy with everything, even if I have to murder the Commandant to stop his escapade. If that's what he really wants.

The soldiers in the truck I rode in tried to ease the tension that engulfed everyone by telling jokes but I just couldn't blend with their mood. The thought of Ajuma filled my mind, how was she surviving? What sort of hard time is my brother subjecting her to? And what does the shameless Commandant want with Nancy? All these three thoughts kept me miles apart from my other colleagues in the truck.

We soon arrived at the point where some Ecomog troops had been stationed waiting for reinforcement. We all alighted and we were ordered to split into units of six squad, and each squad with a specified task.

One of my colleagues was armed with a sophisticated Dard 120 rocket launcher, we were soon allotted our flank. Heavy mortar guns were stationed behind us to provide the necessary backup when the need arises but now we were expected to advance while holding our fire, and can only shoot when we come under rebel attack, we were also ordered to maintain radio silence.

I took all I considered important with me including extra magazines, and My sophisticated automatic rifle stayed firm in my hands. After about an hour of advancing, I took my turn to lead the rest squad through a strange land I have never ventured before.

The terrain was rocky and dense, I stayed close to the ground as much as possible, bushes and tree branches slapped me as I punched my way through the dense jungle, strange insects and rodents would make me freeze intermittently, I led the way for about forty minutes without any serious incident except for the occasional harassment from rodents and strange insects who's territory we invaded with impunity as we pushed through the jungle,.

I retreated to the middle of the squad when I was relieved by the next soldier who took over the lead, we kept pushing through the dense shrubs without any confrontation, our objective was to take the RUF rebels stationed at Makeni by surprise and attempt to dislodge them from their stronghold,

The fourth soldier leading the squad continued pushing through the dense shrubs and the rest of the squad followed his trail cautiously, we occasionally paused to look at the special map provided for the mission and compass so we don't stray into the hands of the enemies.

Twenty minutes after the fourth soldier took over the lead, we heard a loud snap of a metal trap under a thick undergrowth, the trap narrowly missed the right foot of the soldier leading the squad by a few inches, our footsteps on the dense grasses had propped a rabbit out of hiding and it unknowingly ran into the metal trap and triggered it, the trap severed the rabbit into two, the leading soldier quickly called for a halt, " God!, I narrowly escaped been caught, he said with a shaky voice. He was emotionally shaken by the close shave, as a result he was asked to fall back by the Squad leader and a fifth soldier was asked to take the lead.

Our movement became slower afterward. When it was my turn to lead the group again, I knew danger was getting closer by every step of the way, the forest was very humid and warm, and sweat began to drip down my forehead. I was taking each step with absolute caution. One could still hear the exchange of gun fire echoing in the distance. Suddenly I heard a tree branch snap, it made my heart skipped a beat. I quickly swung and faced the direction of the sound, an Africa Mamba snake landed on the fourth soldier on the queue, the snake fell off the broken tree branch, his rifle suddenly fell off the soldier's hand dropped on the ground when the snake landed on his head, and he quickly wrestled the snake off his head in desperation. Somehow, no shot was fired during the ensuing confusion, the snake succeeded in wiggling into the surrounding shrubs without any bruise. When the confusion was over and no one was hurt we giggled silently and continued our match toward Makeni.

There was no other incident along the way as we pushed through the dense jungle except a few encounter with animals who are residence of the jungle, as we match on we came across to a diamond mining field, and we halted our match about half a kilometer to the open field.

We all took strategic position around the mine field and our Dard 120 rocket launcher was mounted on a high spot by the soldier carrying it. While we all waited for events to unfold in the mine, I could spot various mining activities going on in and around the open mine field, From a distance I saw some RUF rebels manning some automatic machine gun mounted on tripods facing various directions to provide protection for their illegal mining activities. I wondered why this part of the rebels' territory was unmarked by anyone. This mine field was a clandestine revenue spinner for the RUF.

I looked around me carefully for a perfect cover to pitch my head, I soon spotted a log of tree that was covered by termites mud, the log must have been several year old there. I took my position under the log of wood, allowing it to serve as cover for my head, I laid beside the log, while others took various position they considered safe for them, from my position the activities going on in the distance field was very glaring, soon an idea struck my mind, if we succeed in pushing the rebels away. I will pocket some diamonds, I thought, enough to give me plenty of money to enable me settle down with Ajuma when am able to redeploy back to Nigeria, I thought of how we would both relocate to a nice place and start a fantastic life style there. My day dreaming was brought to an abrupt end by an explosion far to my right side, the distance blast shocked everyone almost to their heels, and then there was a brief silence again. One of my colleague who had earlier sort for cover on top of a nearby tree, suddenly whispered, ''someone has stepped on a mine, someone has stepped on a mine, our man is down'' he was suddenly cut short by an outburst of machine gun fire.

The rebels had noticed our presence and had started shooting sporadically in panic; but no shot was fired toward our direction so we didn't return any fire either. From my position I could see the rebels rushing out to boost their frontlines. The shooting grew intense with time but no shot was fired toward my position, soon saw grenade hitting various rebel targets but a dense forest obstructed my view of other ECOMOG soldiers in my squad,

I could judge that our colleagues were not finding things easy. Suddenly, we heard footfalls running towards us in the bush from behind. The rebels were reacting to the outbreak of fighting in the area with a very vicious force. They were rushing to the front to reinforce their position through where we had pitched out tent. Unknown to the rebels they kept "Crushing tall grasses and heading towards us. I quickly adjusted my position, so that my body could be well covered by the log, and my colleagues also did the same for better cover. The event turned out to be one of the most successful ambush I have ever undertaken.

They were completely ignorant that we had secured the entire area, and they ran into our ambush. The rebels numbering about seventy dashed towards us, as they advance towards us, my heart kept pounding like a locomotive engine and I kept shifting my rifle from one target to the other without pulling my trigger, apparently confusion on the right target as there were so many to choose from, every part of my body stayed motionless except for my hands. The rebels were about fifty meters away. My mind was on red alert as I waited for the rocket to fire and signal return of fire and disperse the rebels

The soldier on the tree top fired his rocket into the midst of the advancing rebels, and we immediately followed with burst of machine gun firing toward the direction which the rocket struck the rebels.

The identities of the rebels were as vivid as a full moon, from what I saw of the rebels, they were mostly young boy except for a few young adults among their rank, I felt very sorry for shooting those young boys but I had no choice. I either shoot them or they will kill or amputate me, Then Sule's ordeal suddenly came to my mind. Then sudden madness griped me. "This is pay back day" I yelled, as I fired relentlessly, even when it became apparent that the rebels were only able to fire some few aimless shots that didn't make any difference, I kept firing.

After about ten minutes, none of the rebels were left standing or running, it was a massacre of some sort. By now some shot were already coming toward our direction from the mining field. Our rocket launcher continued to hitting rebel targets and our focus was geared at the field once more.

As the fighting raged on, Ecomog's heavy mortar started landing shells on the mining field. I wondered who called for the shelling support, the shelling provided us the cover and time to choose our targets carefully, after about forty minutes of fierce fighting, the population of the rebels diminished drastically.

I saw some of our men scattered on the far flank of the mining field attempting to harass the rebels out of their trenches. Shell kept landing intermittently on the field sending dust and objects flying into the air; some of which were human flesh. Smell of roasted flesh and smoke filled our nostrils. Each time I turned and looked around me to be sure no enemy was creeping behind me.

When the heavy shelling subsided the remaining rebels had no choice but to raise their white piece of cloth to signify surrender. I felt like jumping for joy, but I quickly controlled my emotions gradually, calm started to return to the battle ground. I maintained my position and watched how some of our men filed the surrendering rebels on a straight line. All their guns and weapon were gathered at a point some of my colleagues came out and match toward the mining field, the first man that led the way from our flank mistakenly stepped on a mine triggering an explosion in the process, from where I laid on the ground, I saw how he was blown apart by the blast. The explosion triggered a few panic gun fire from some of our men, but calm soon returned again when the cause of the explosion became clear.

I stood up and together with the remaining of my colleagues I led the way towards the field through a narrow path in the bush. The track led us safely into the field without any incident, the blown apart remain of humans littered the ground. Spent bullets and empty shells dotted the field and it gave a clear account of the level of military operation that had just taken place, with my right hand gripping my rifle tightly, I careful walked around the field to help gather abandoned weapons.

I had spent awhile on the mining field helping to gathering weapons, I stumbled on a bullet riddled body, he looked very much like the oldest man I have seen so far among the rebels on the mine. I decided to search his bulging pocket, and I bent over his body and trusted my hand into his blood soaked trouser pocket. My hand touched some hard pebbles, I guessed they were raw diamonds. Without a second thought, I quickly scooped and shoved the pebble like objects into my pocket and quickly moved away from the corpse.

Yes my plans are working out better than anticipated I thought. This stones could fetch me millions of naira back home. My hands were becoming shaky. I had never probed a dead man before, the blood soaked corpse gave me a strange creepy sensation.

The prisoners of war [the arrested RUF rebels] were escorted to the Ecomog heavy artillery position far behind the diamond mining field for onward transfer to Ecomog detention center, some of the arrested rebels sustained various degrees of serious injuries and I wondered if some of them will ever survive, I kept myself busy as much as I could, while maintaining a very high degree of alertness. Frogs and the combined choruses of insects interlude the brief silence but in the distances occasional sounds of explosion and gun fire interrupted the melodious sounds of nature.

After a few moments of roaming around the field and its surrounding area. I decided to settle down on a sand filled drum beside a tall shrubs that act as fence for the field at the left flank. There I was able to have a conspicuous view of the entire field except for a few surrounding hills, some Ecomog soldiers had already maintained a strategic positions around the mining field, the entire area was securely guarded by the soldiers, the mining has been one of RUF major source of revenue and it was also of strategic importance to the rebels.

As I rested on the field I wondered how much my loot could worth, each time I felt my pocket to be sure the diamonds were still there. The exact human strength of our presence on the field was unknown to me but I could spot our men scattered around the field and its surrounding areas. I spent a few minutes examining my rifle to be sure it was still in perfect order.

My mind kept wondering about various issues centered on the two women in my life, Ajuma and Nancy, my mind was worried about them anytime I was not thinking of how to stay alive or escape the attack of the rebels. I seemed to think less about my parents and siblings. My mind suddenly shifted to the Commandant, how could that Commandant be so callous and cruel to have thought of flirting with Nancy despite the load of women at his disposal, I just couldn't imagine him messing up with Nancy right under my nose. The thought of keeping Nancy happy without having any sexual relationship with her gave me even great concern. My desire to genuinely help Nancy without exploiting her weakness kept flashing across my mind.

I soon found myself dozing off so I took another posture that enabled me to rest my head properly on the sand-filled drum while my body stretched out on the ground as if I was taking a cover. Our Team Leader shouted a couple of orders I didn't quite understand. I ignored it and prayed briefly for God's protection and thereafter dozed off.

I was jerked out of sleep by an outburst of machine gun fire, I had no idea of what the time was but I knew it was late into the night. Fatigue had forced some of my colleagues manning the hilly front, to doze off allowing the rebels to infiltrate the mining fields.

I jumped up and grabbed my rifle for a brief moment I was confused on what next to do, but I didn't know what the problem was or what to fire at. The sound of machine gun fire over shadowed the cool night air. I opened fire on some men advancing toward my position I concluded were rebels, those who were not hit by the hail of bullets I fired toward them hastily retreated.

The sand filled drum absorbed many bullets fired toward my position. The fighting raged on amidst confusion and uncertainty. The battle soon degenerated into a one on one encounter on the hilly terrain. This made it very fatal to shoot indiscriminately. The night sky lighted the field, but the darkness still maintained its supremacy.

I soon found out that more rebels where taking up prominent positions in and around the field, while shooting continued relentlessly. I considered my cover to be very safe and comfortable so I had refused to make any advance or retreat from that spot, the spot gave me a very good position to hit many good targets but after striking several targets and preventing any advance by the rebels on my position something suddenly happened. A huge tree branch struck my rifle from behind. The impact was unexpected, as the rifle fell off my hand, I quickly rolled over and I saw a huge dark tall figure of about six feet swinging a tree branch straight at me, I had to rollover again to avoid the man trying to violently struck me with a big tree branch, he viciously tried to knock me dead with the tree branch as if he was trying to kill a poisonous snake.

With the aid of my combat boots, I dealt out a devastating kick that struck the man's tibia, I heard him groan in pain, and as if he was in confusion as to whether to remain standing or sit on the ground, I capitalized on his state of confusion and surged toward where my gun fell, but I didn't reach the rifle before the man grabbed and pulled my leg violently. I threw a few aimless kick at him with my other leg, but I found myself under the man's heavy weight, the man was huge and muscular and it seemed like he weighed a ton.

As a result of the excruciating weight I found myself carrying. I tried to turn his weight over but my force fell short of requirements to achieve my aim. The man's palm moved suddenly to grip my wind pipe but I grabbed his hand and for a moment we flex our muscles. He was a very strong man I must admit, after a brief struggle he succeeded in grabbing my throat, his grip was like that of a steel vice, and he aggressively size my wind pipe sapping me of vital oxygen. It suddenly occurred to me that the man meant to suffocate me, I started to struggle for my live, within seconds I felt my eyes were bulging out of it socket, the pains became very severe and unbearable, I suddenly realize that this man has the cruel intension to strangle me. I was completely helpless under the man's weight and I felt my live was fast diminishing, everything flashed across my mind, my mother, father, brothers, sister, Ajuma and nice Nancy,

It all seemed to me like a trance, here I am losing my life for the sake of another man's greed, and I considered the deadly grip on my wind pipe by the man as a cruel attempt to strangulate me. I struggled to free myself, I suddenly felt a stings on my ear and shoulder. I suddenly realized they were soldier ants and without further hesitation. I grabbed the soil around where my head rested and threw it at the man's face. I repeated the action three times and hoped for the grip on my throat to loosen. Soon the man's grip loosened around my wind pipe as he tried to slap the ants off his face.

I quickly took a deep breath, and lifted my chest up while the man was still squatting on my lap. And with all the strength I had left in me, I punched and push the man, I quickly struggled to my knees and hastily looked around for my gun, but darkness had enveloped everywhere and didn't give me any sense of visibility, I quickly realized the man was already staggering towards me when I picked up the tree branch. I aimed a swing at the man's head, he didn't see the branch coming when it struck his head, and I heard him yell in pain as he went down on his knees and grabbed his head for succor. The force I used tossed me of balance and I struggled to regain my stability.

The man got to his feet faster than I had ever expected and dashed towards me. This time I made another swing with the branch toward the advancing man who bent over and I missed my target, I soon found myself losing balance and crashing to the ground. I quickly rolled off missing his kick by an inch. I rolled over again, and I felt my left hand touched my gun. And I succeeded in picking up my rifle and positioning the gun, as the man dashed towards me, I pulled the trigger. The shot had barely gone off when the man's massive body landed on me. I thought the bullet didn't hit the man but when his warm blood and intestine touched my skin, I was relieved I had hit the target. He struggle before finally slumping on me, I pushed his massive body away from mine. And I laid on the ground still. The sting of ants jolted me up, I stood up dropped my gun and slapped the ants off my face, and body. When I was done, I then realized I was soaked in blood with bits of human flesh sticking to my camouflage. Keeping low to avoid flying bullets, I striped off my camouflage jacket leaving me with just a green T shirt. Feeling much worn out, I grabbed my machine gun that now weighed like a ton in my hand and crawled towards the path where I had entered the field from previously. The blast of gun fire and occasional explosions still remained intense. When I crawled for about seventy meter into the jungle, it suddenly occurred to me that my diamonds were in the jacket I had removed and dropped behind. I became motionless and I immediately turned back to retrieve my jacket.

The actual position of Ecomog troop was not clear to me but I refused to be bothered. When I got where my jacket was, the shooting had begun to gradually subside. A husky voice was shouting orders. I didn't need a prophet to tell me that the man was the rebel commander, he was doling out orders to his fighters I quickly put on the jacket and grabbed my gun and started crawling back the way I came. I succeeded in getting into the forest but with difficulties.

While in the forest I was confused on which direction to go. As I stood for a brief moment, puzzled, suddenly a very bright light flashed into my eyes blinding me for some seconds. "Hold it and drop your gun," a voice ordered, I stood still raising up my hand in surrender and tried to look away from the light but it kept following my face as I shifted it. Without any hesitation, I dropped my rifle, and raised my hands above my head, I saw a small boy of about six years old picked up my rifle, he could hardly carry the rifle because the weight of the rifle is almost proportional to his own body mass, he disappeared into the darkness, then somebody from behind gave me a vicious push after trapping my feet with his, I slammed into the bush and my hands were immediately tied behind my back with a speed I never thought possible, It then dawned on me that I have been capture by the enemy.

We trekked for hours in silence and yet the distance seemed endless, the diamond mine had fallen to the rebels again I thought, Ecomog's soldiers resistance didn't match the rebel's exploits. Thirteen ragtag boys and girls between the ages of six and fifteen and four terribly wounded Ecomog soldiers were matched further into the jungle along with me. I became so tired I felt like collapsing, my fastened hand created more difficulty for me.

We got to a place where a small but fast running stream flowed across our path, the four wounded soldiers were almost as good as dead. They had lost so much blood without any medical attention. I couldn't quite get the actual number of rebels that guarded us but I'm sure they we well above fifty in number, fully armed and fierce looking. Some in their teens and others in their early twenties, they had been well groomed to kill without mercy, even their own parents.

I was put in front of the remaining prisoners of war, I followed the leading batch of rebels into the stream, I was just half way across the stream that swallowed up to my waist when a gunshot rented the air, I stiffen and quickly turned around to know if we were been executed, the head of one of my Ecomog unit had been blown apart by bullets from one of the rebels fire.

The soldier had refused to cross the stream and he was shot in the head. Without any hesitation the rest prisoners ran into the stream. "Move bastard," a voice ordered, I promptly complied. When I was out of the stream, I felt some insect-like stings, I could not slap off the insect because my hands were tied behind my back, I had to bear the pains as it emanated from different part of my skin,

Soon after everyone had crossed the stream, I had a girl cry out for help. Suddenly we all turned to see what had happened to her, but darkness denied us a clear view, her cry grew wild and several of the other girls joined in the wailing. When all the threats of the rebels couldn't stop their crying, a flash light was pointed at one of the girl, what I saw sent chills down my spine.

Leeches were all over their bodies, I quickly realize that some have found their way into my trouser from the torn parts. The sight triggered me into trying to wiggle free to beat off the blood sucking insects but the strength of the rope prevented me. Somehow, the girls freed themselves from the blood sucking insects with the help of some of the RUF rebels, but mine kept sucking my blood.

The three remaining wounded soldiers also managed to free themselves of the insects as they were left untied due to their injuries. I found it very difficult to walk properly due to the pains and irritation the leeches were inflicting on me. I dragged my feet along the bushy path and occasionally, I attempted to use one of my leg to rub against the other if that will be able to shake the leeches off my skin, I was not even sure if it works.

Several minute after we left the stream another of the wounded Ecomog soldier slumped. After losing so much blood, he had no strength left in him. "Lazy man, move," one of the rebels yelled, But the soldier could not respond, "shoot him, he is wasting our time" the husky voice of the RUF Leader ordered, shots suddenly rang out in compliance to the order.

When we finally got to the rebels base in the town of Makeni, we were ordered into a heavily guarded compound, there I saw children that had been adopted and are being groomed into having wild conception. I stood on a spot for a while looking around me like a hen in search of where to roost. The fear of been amputated started to encapsulate my ambition, and what if the pebble like the diamond were a found on me? I would be promptly executed, I thought. Miraculously, I have not been searched.

I choose to settle down beside a bereaved little girl in a dark corner of the compound. "How are you," I greeted the girl as mild as I could amidst my tensed and stressed saturated mind, she declined to respond, "please, I need your help," I pleaded, "what?" She asked, sounding more like a cartoon character, "insects are biting me, help me, my legs," I pleaded, she quietly crawled closer to me and she perfectly pilled the leeches off my skin and crushing them one after the other in the process, each time my blood will pop out of the insect abdomen, I presumed the leeches must have sucked several pints of my blood. "Thank you very much" I said in a relieved tone. "What is your name," I asked, "Gladys," she answered, shifting slightly away from me, "can you help me remove this rope?" I asked, turning to show her the rope that was used to tie me. Just as I felt her hand touch the rope on my hand, a voice called out, "Hey! Hey!! Where is that man?" I quickly turned to the opposite direction. Suddenly a flash light lit my face in the dark. "you! Come here," the voice ordered.

I struggled up my feet and followed the man, we walked pass several makeshift structures before reaching a fairly large hall, my mind was preoccupied with the thought of amputation, The RUF rebels were renowned for being notorious in the maiming of their captives, could this be how I will lose my limb? I thought.

I was led in by four guards armed with pump action machine guns. The hall has tattered walls made of rusty roofing sheets on one side and bullets ridden wall on the other side. I was matched straight to a man in his middle age, dark in complexion, tall and skinny, I later knew he was General Samuel Bakare alias General Mosquito. The vicious murderer now assumed the leadership of the Revolutionary United Front Rebels.

"Untie him," Gen. Mosquito ordered, I was quickly untied by one of his body guard with a shaky hand, sit down Ecomog soldier, Gen. Mosquito ordered in his husky vicious voice. I was so scared I began to sweat profusely, what if this diamond pebbles are found on me, how do I explain it, I thought. "Thank you sir," I said, and sat directly opposite him. Welcome to my jungle Mr. Ecomog he continued, hesitated, "what is your name?" He asked, "you can call me Reuben if you don't mind sir," I politely cut in, "Are you not an Ecomog invading soldier?"

He asked, I kept quiet and looked at his face, he then continued, "My friend, you have no option than to corporate and live, or disagree and die a slow painful death with your friends, So what do you think my good friend, he said with a clinched teeth and fist.

I don't understand what you mean Sir, I replied, if I explain to you and you refuse to cooperate, you know you must die with your colleagues. Don't bother to explain then, I can't help you in anyway. I cut in suddenly, I thought it was all over for me, there was no need subjecting myself to any further anguish, I thought.

It's like you don't know who you are dealing with. Gen. Mosquitoes said snapping his finger and before I could utter a word, four men descended on me, dragging me out of my seat, I was subjected to several minutes of beating. After what seemed like having a date with the devil that lasted for about twenty minutes; I was left with a swollen and battered head. I laid on the floor with blood trickling down different parts of my body, "Mr. Ecomog you have just received our VIP treatment, I hope your testicles are not broken," Gen. Mosquito said with a jeering voice, I didn't say anything, he then continued, "have you decide to cooperate or you want to be shown around a little before you play the game with the mighty General Mosquito?" There was a brief silence, as I groan in extreme pain, "are you playing or not? We have no time to waste my friend," Gen. Mosquito said harshly, I remained silent, he walked close to me and without hesitation he snapped his finger twice and I was immediately dragged out of the hall to another smaller room with fresh blood stains on the walls, I was dragged to the center of the hall. The men, numbering about eight didn't ask me any questions as they went about their murderous duties without mercy, moments after I was brought into the hall One of my captured colleagues was dragged into the hall and pushed violently against the wall, "What is the matter, Haba! Yankuri! Mana!" The soldier pleaded in a frightened northern Nigerian Hausa accent.

The soldier had barely finished his pleas when an automatic rifle sprayed out bullets just behind me striking the soldier several times on his torso. He dropped on the floor in the pool of his blood lifelessly. It happened so quickly, I was engulfed by fear when suddenly another small girl was dragged into the hall followed by a young boy in his early teens with a huge cutlass on his right hand. The poor girl wept all along, "God, this people must be insane," I thought.

The girl was brought right in front of me, she stood in front of me with her tears soaked eyes. "give her a short sleeve," one of the men ordered in a vicious tone, and without any hesitation the boy waved his machetes and struck the girls right hand from the elbow region, several times. The amputated hand was held up by the rebel who did the amputation

Blood gushed out uncontrollably from the girl's hand, she wailed in absolute agony, and excruciating pain as tears began to flow out of my eyes. "Take her to the clinic to stop the bleeding," the voice ordered, this is crazy, absolute madness, I thought. Could it be my turn next? "Okay, move, the General will like to have a word with you," a husky voice ordered, I hesitated as I watched the little girl been dragged out to their so-called clinic, within minutes, I was also dragged by my jacket collar to General. Mosquito's presence.

"You can sit down, I hope you enjoyed the great spectacle my men treated you to?" General Mosquito said in a jeering voice, I kept silent, I was still soaked in grief about what I just saw, "Where you've just been to is our area of entertainment and more of your colleagues will be executed there, and your head will be bashed open with an iron rod there, if you don't join my team now." Gen. Mosquito reaffirmed, I looked around me saying nothing, the blood drunk rebels stood around me as if they were waiting for the order to cut me open.

At some point, fear enveloped me, "you can't do worse than killing me and my friends but some day very soon, you will be stopped by death too," I lashed out angrily, "you will be doing lot of harm to your brothers and yourself if you don't accept my offer, I will pay you tenfold of what your country is paying you presently and you will have plenty of diamonds. I know you already have some in your pocket," General Mosquito replied, My mind raced back to the diamond I went back to collect that led to my been captured, fear suddenly filled me and I looked at myself briefly and felt extremely dejected.

The blood stain on me had caked and I was smelling like a decomposing corpse already, "search him," Gen. Mosquitoes ordered, two lanky young men step forward and one of them seized and dragged me out of the chair while the other ran his hands over my body in no time he brought out everything in my pocket including the piece of diamonds, he placed everything on Gen. Mosquito's desk. ''Good! Good!! You all disguise as peace keepers to steal our diamonds ah! You will see,'' General Mosquito jeered, ''keep him in the lodge till tomorrow,'' He ordered, ''by then I will decide what to do to you, if you don't cooperate, I will make you smoke your tail,'' his facial posture suddenly turned fierce. ''Nothing can find its way out of my grip,'' he warned. I felt so guilty like never before.

I offered no resistance to my being pushed violently out of Gen. Mosquito presence. It was beginning to approach dawn. I was taken past many heavily guarded compound before finally arriving at a lowly fenced compound. The door was swung open by one of the waiting guard. I was dragged inside violently.

The yard was fully equipped with various torture apparatus. Blood rushed to my face in great fear and I started sweating profusely, I could clearly hear sounds of matching feet and various orders been barked out from the distance. Very faint sounds of gun fire and explosions occasionally interfered with the regular sounds of insects.

Without the exchange of any word, I was hanged with my two hands. They all left me in the yard dangling in excruciating pain. The pain forced me to cry out for help but without any help coming my way I soon slumped into a coma.

I was awoken by the morning sun, whose ray beamed into my eyes as I laid on the ground of the heavily guarded compound. Everything became very difficult and painful to do. My breath was seriously inadequate and I felt like my death had begun to manifest, I was still deliberating on my fate, whether, I was alive or dead, when I was ordered up, I remained motionless, deliberating if I will be unable to move any part of my body.

I laid still on the ground then the owner of the voice that had been yelling orders stepped into the yard, he was dressed in an all-black outfit with a yellow gallon on his left hand. Without saying anything, he emptied the content of the gallon on my body, at first the liquid soothed my pains, then suddenly felt as if I was on fire. The effect of the liquid on my body was beyond description. The terrible effect of the liquid made me jump on my feet suddenly, I was between insanity and death.

My reaction triggered an out bust of laughter, among the rebels that had gathered behind the fence to watch the funfair. Only God can explain what the liquid was made off. I slammed my body on the ground and wriggled on the ground in an inexplicable condition for a long time, before I was dragged out of the yard while the men continued to laugh wildly as if they were watching the Bill Cosby show.

We met General. Mosquito laughing when we got to where he stood, "Yes! You should be able to talk now Mr. Reuben, I want you to lead RUF into Freetown," he paused briefly, "are you going to join us or not," he yelled, "yes Sir," came out of my mouth suddenly without any hesitation. "Good!! I can see you can't discuss comfortably now, release him and allow him take a bath," One of the guards handed an empty bucket, a sponge made of dried grass and a tablet of locally made black soap, it was as if they had prepared all the items for me. I was shown a shallow well where I hurriedly fetch water, I was so excited and I just couldn't wait for the water to touch my aching body.

Half way into my bath, I saw a clean military style uniform hanging where I had hung my filthy uniform. After my bath, my entire body was relieved of most of the afflictions. I dressed up in the new uniform as soon as I had finished my bath and was led back to Gen. Mosquito, he softened up a bit when he saw me coming, and parted his lips in a brief vicious smile, but I kept a straight expressionless face as I pulled a nearby wooden chair closer and I sat in front of him, "are you alright, at least alright enough to start work?" General Mosquito asked, "before I will do anything for you, my colleagues should be treated," I urged, "yes that reminds me," Gen. Mosquito said snapping his finger, one of his body guard stepped out, you have to take those men to see the doctor. Tell doctor they are my guest. Gen. Mosquito ordered.

When the guard he beckoned stepped forward, he continued, "your friends will now be taken good care of," General Mosquito said, for a moment, he stared at the roof of what served as his office briefly and he then pulled out his drawer and brought out a map and spread it on his desk. He briefly acquainted me with the map details. "can I call you Reuben?" he asked and without waiting for my response, he continued "I want you to tell me where Ecomog are stationed and where they are laying ambush for my men, General. Mosquito asked, I looked at him thoughtfully and then the map, "but how do you want me to remember all that?" ' "you will point out the black spots, it's up to you," Gen. Mosquito yelled, "you have my word," I said, as I picked up the map and buried my head into it, I studied the map for just a few minutes when suddenly shots rang out, I was startled and I quickly stood up. "sit down my friend and continue your work, the gun shot is none of your business. Gen. Mosquito ordered. I had barely sat on the chair, when one of the rebels dashed into where I and Gen. Mosquito were, and yelled "Sir, the Ecomog soldiers who were arrested yesterday tried to escape on their way to the clinic, they killed two of our men, before we killed one of them and arrested others, the RUF rebel said in a gasp.

I became very restless, "good! Good!! I will come and see the situation myself later," Gen. Mosquito said, dismissing the shabby looking man, "General, should I come with you?" I pleaded, "it's not necessary the situation is under control," General Mosquito replied as he walked out of the hall, I quickly stood up and walked toward the exit. But I was confronted by six heavily armed men who ordered me back in side. I immediately obey without any hesitation.

I stared at the map blankly not able to comprehend anything, about fifteen minutes later, I heard footsteps coming into the shabby hall, I hastily drew two circles on the map and quickly wore the look of a no-nonsense officer who was believed to have made a startling discovery, I pretended to be ignorant of any ones presence. General Mosquito was accompanied by one of his top field commander into the hall,

General Mosquito walked straight to his chair and sat there, "One of your friend had to die for his foolishness and I am still considering whether to cut off the hands of your remaining friends so they don't pose any threat here again. Gen. Mosquito said calmly, "General, you waste too much time, the men are useless to us, we shouldn't waste time eliminating them," his aid said, "But this our friend here will not be happy if we do that," Gen. Mosquito replied, "how have you gone my friend?" Gen. Mosquito continued, peeping to see where I had circle on the map, "so your men are deployed in these areas?" Gen. Mosquito asked in a jeering manner, "yes Sir, I am sure we have soldiers stationed around those areas," I said, "what's their strength like?" Gen. Mosquito asked, "I am not very sure of the strength but I am sure the units are backed by heavy artilleries and helicopter gun support. is very well at their disposal, I replied, "We are not afraid of any encounter with Ecomog, all I know is that we must over run Freetown soon, very soon," Gen. Mosquito reaffirmed, then there was a brief pause, "Reuben keep the map aside for a while let me introduce you to some of my commanders," Gen. Mosquito said, I felt very relieved to be away from the map.

I quickly folded the map and joined Gen. Mosquito and the man who came with him who also happened to be one of his commanders, I was led alongside groups of young fighters brandishing automatic rifles.

Gen Mosquito walked past many feeble structures used to hold detainees and supplies. When we got to the shade of a hug tree, we waited there for the remaining commanders to be summoned. We waited in silence, everyone staring at different directions in a state of confusion.

Several minutes later, the commanders arrived under the huge tree, They all stamped their foot in salute, slowly waving his right hand General Mosquito introduced me as a "Necessary Commander Reuben was a member of the Nigeria Army but he has now decided to team up with the RUF to fight the Government of Ahmed Tijan Kabba and to bring justice, peace and progress to Sierra-Leone, and to destroyer rouges and rapist claiming to be fighting for justice," Peace and progress indeed, I thought.

After he spoke, I stretched out my hand and shook the hands of all the rebel commanders. "Commander. Reuben you may go back to work, I will join you later," I turned and gave a military styled salute and headed back without any hesitation. But to my surprise I was escorted by ten heavily armed rebels.

We soon arrived at the shabby hall which served as the office of Gen. Mosquito and the rebel logistic section. For the very first time I decided to ignore the presence of the gun trotting guards to concentrate on doing my best to preserve my live, I knew my time was limited, from where I sat, I carefully observed the entire hall for objects of interested, my gaze paid off when I spotted a satellite telephone set, neatly concealed among books on a book shelf beside a bullet riddle wall.

I quickly looked away from that direction to avoid any suspicious from the guards and started making notes of advice and strategies on how to best tackle the Ecomog troops and at the same time creating loop holes to trap the rebels, the day was gruesome as having a vacation in hell, General Mosquito didn't come back to see me that same day, and at dusk a man entered the hall and said he was instructed to lead me to my lodge, without hesitation considering my bored state of mind, I hastily packed up and followed him as he led the way followed by my guards. I was anxious to lay my head to sleep for the first time in many days, maybe with this sleep, I thought, I might get more relief from the pain battling for prominence in my body. The trip to my so called lodge was quiet with lots of uncertainty. We finally arrived at the lodge, the lodge was a block of one room apartments, with two entrance in opposite directions, the corridor that separated the entrance to the apartments had rolls of benches I didn't know what they were meant for, and I was ushered into the room that was second to the last on the right. The apartment was neat, and well kept, it's dimly illuminated by a blue bulb functioning from electricity generated by a small generator outside the building. A medium sized bed sat at the left side of the room with a small cupboard, beside it. The arrangement looked okay to me, ''your food will be ready soon sir,'' the usher said, that announcement pushed saliva to my mouth, I quickly took off my shoes and laid on the bed, as the usher shut the door, the feeling of hunger griped my stomach as I laid flat on the bed, waiting for the food to come in earnestly, soon the door swung open and the usher brought in a tray which he laid on the table, ''thank you,'' I said, he bowed and left me alone, I quickly pounced on the tray, opening all the stainless bowls on the tray, I was served a meal of corn and cassava starch with vegetable soup stuffed with smoked tilapia fish in no time, I finished devouring the meal that tasted very salty.

I was working on the skeleton of the fish with my teeth when the door pushed open again, this time six girls between the ages of nine and thirteen accompanied the usher into the apartment, "Sir, here are some beautiful ladies for you to choose from Sir, some might still be virgin, the usher said smiling like a jack pot winner. My month stopped chewing and hung open in disbelieve and disgust, "you call this ladies? Or what did I just hear you say? I yelled after a brief moment of silence the girls were innocent looking and frightened, "For God's sake, take this girls back to their parents," The girls were then ushered out, I felt sorry for those kids, my mind remained restless about the fate of those girls.

The usher entered the apartment just moments after I had stretched out on the bed for a snap, This time the usher came in with four women that reminded me of the kwashiorkor stricken children of Ethiopia in the nineteen eighties, Before he could say a word, I angrily asked what are all these for? Our guest don't sleep alone here, since you rejected those girls that they are under age, I had to bring you your choice, the usher explain, God, did I ever tell you what my choice was? I pleaded, I just couldn't imagine myself laying side by side with any human of these women that have lost all the attribute of a healthy he brought into the apartment calling them women. "Am obeying an order for our guest not to sleep alone here," the usher said, I shook my head in disbelieve, the women kept staring at me as our conversation progressed. After a brief hesitation, "alright, you then bring back the girls, I retorted, "sorry sir, those girls have already been booked after you rejected them," the usher said, what do you mean by that? I asked. "The girls are with other guests already," he said as he started clearing the tray from the table.

He turned to leave the room, I became apprehensive, "wait! You can't leave these things here," I said pointing to the women standing right opposite the bed where I laid, Sir, "make your choice while I put this tray away, I will soon be back," The usher said and walked away.

I became confused and angry at the same time, this women I thought, are sure visa to AIDS and HIV infections.

My mouth was still open and my head nodding in disbelieve, when the door opened and the usher walked in, "Sir, have you made your choice," he asked, I kept quiet, "and if not," he continued, "I have another option waiting outside," Without any hesitation, "you better bring in your other options I said and he waved the women outside and four men walked in together replacing the women, I was thrown into an even greater confusion. The usher kept quite while one of the men who was more heavily built, with muscles protruded out of his unbuttoned jacket move towards me, look here, no one breaks the law here, and these are your last option, pointing to the shabbily dressed men standing opposite me. If I may ask, what should I do with this men, I asked curiously, you must make love to them or you will be forced to make love to a dog or goat, the man said furiously! What? I shouted, you are all mad here. Yes, that is why we are called the RUF rebels. I looked around me helplessly, if that is the case, call back those women, I pleaded. He hesitated them ordered the men out of the apartment, and minutes later, one of the skinny woman stepped into the apartment, my heart skipped a beat when I saw her.

The muscular man drew the woman closer and whispered something to her and he walked out. Good evening Sir, the woman greeted, I couldn't believe what was happening I refused to respond to her greeting, I wore a scornful look, staring at her as I sat on the bed resting my back on the wall, she stepped closer to the bed side and slowly took off her blouse revealing her flabby breasts.

The sight irritated me to the extreme. As she made the move to unbutton her skirt I turned and buried my face into the wall. Soon I felt her climb the bed and started caressing my back. I stiffened in anguish. She made several attempt to turn my body to face her but I resisted. When she didn't succeed, she then laid her stinky scrawny body on mine, I just couldn't imagine the disgust that ran through my spine, and about an hour later, during which I had started sweating, an outburst of automatic gun fire broke the silence of the night, I jolted in shock and loud footsteps started walking in the corridor. They will come here and shoot us if you don't make love to me.

The woman said in a shaky voice. Fear suddenly gripped me displacing all my hatred without question. I turned and grab the woman and pulled her under me. The foot step drew closer and the door of my apartment suddenly swung open, I quickly started trusting my waist in a love making manner with my trousers on. I didn't see the man who stepped into the room because I didn't look, as I pretended to be wild in love making. The women also clinched to me caressing my body with her shaky bony hands. The door remained open for some minutes before it was gently shut by the intruder.

Sweat covered my entire body. The feeling of what I was doing made me sick, moments after the door closed, I eased myself of the woman and laid beside her with my eye closed. I unstrapped my belt and laid motionless. I heard the footsteps walking out of the corridor and later faded away.

Hours later, I decided to look at what had become of the woman, what I saw frightened me and I hurriedly turned away, she was stark naked, her mouth hung open and in deep slumber, at that point I started praying for sleep to give me a temporary relief from the nightmare. I was experiencing.

I was awaken by sporadic machine gun fire, I quickly rolled off the bed and landed on the floor, it sounded like the shots were fired inside the apartment, when the shots died down I stood up to see my manhood sticking out of my trouser, I hurriedly looked at the bed, The woman was no longer there. I looked at my manhood and wondered who could have brought it out, could it be that devilish woman? My apprehension was interrupted by a knock on the door which made me quickly conceal my manhood, before the door swung open, and behind the door was the usher smiling sheepishly at me, " sorry sir, hope you enjoyed your sleep? Your attention is needed by the grand commander, General Mosquito" the usher whispered.

I arrived the hall which served as office for Gen. Mosquito and quickly went to bury my head in the map with my mind drifting from my escape plan to other inhumane mess of hell I found myself in. I decided to circle another spot on the map that will land the rebels in front of one of Ecomog, fieriest mortal range. Moment later, I finished the circling of some spots on the map, and suddenly I heard gun shots rang outside the hall, and in one quick moment my guard ran outside to see what the matter was I ran and grabbed the satellite phone I had spotted previously. I heard the dialing tone when I placed the piece on my ear. I quickly dialed the number of Ecomog headquarters in Freetown. I was only able to say "mayday Rueben on the line," When Gen. Mosquito walked in. in that slit of a second, I manipulated the memory bottom and succeeded in wiping it off. But it was too late for me to replace the handset, General Mosquito already spotted the phone, "are you crazy," he asked angrily. I was only admiring the beauty of the set. I said defending myself, get out from there now, Gen. Mosquitoes ordered. I dropped the receiver and moved away to where I had sat down earlier studying he map. Gen. Mosquito waved his hand to dismiss some of his entourage as I gazed at the man without blinking my eyes pretending to be seriously engaged, I felt the general's eyes on me. "I will pay you a monthly salary of $500, and you will also be entitled to a monthly gift of diamonds if you are loyal to the RUF," he assured, "which other Ecomog out post have you detected," he asked, "two more positions General," I answered, he leaned on the table and stared at where I had circled, without any question, he settled back on his chair a boy walked into the hall carrying a tray, he laid the tray in front of Gen. Mosquitoes. It contained two half-filled high balls and a bottle of red French wine. The boy bowed and left. He raised one of the high balls and then swallowed its content in a gulp and hastily poured another wine into the high ball, "the commanders will soon be here to map out our strategy of over running the capital Freetown, already our forces are making gains on many fronts, the Ecomog are seriously under pressure," he reaffirmed. "That is very good," I said, as I made another circle on the map pretending to be in support of his lunatic quest.

The meeting with the commanders went on as planned, I made several tactical illustrations of how the battle with Ecomog could be won. Before the meeting took off, four strangers were introduced as members of the military junta that seized power. They announced an alliance with the RUF, and with the strength of the two mindless destroyers against the Ecomog, I knew Ecomog will have no antidote to advance their mission in Freetown, unless a miracle happens.

Before the meeting was concluded I was asked by General. Mosquito to excuse them. I was escorted back to my assigned apartment within the rebel territory at about 4:30pm, I ate rice and beans that was kept waiting for me inside my room I stretched on the bed and soon fell into a deep sleep.

I was woken up by the usher who brought my dinner that evening. I ate the food slowly when I was almost through with the food the usher stepped into my room with another set of five little girls of about eight and twelve years old. Without hesitation, I will kept this one, I said pointing to the youngest of the five girls. I felt very sorry for the remaining girls, they would be taken away to face dehumanizing torture in the hands of some shameless men at such a tender age, I thought. The usher helped cleared the table and advised the remaining girls to leave the room. I was soon left alone with the girl, I laid on the bed imagining what fate the others will be facing in the hands of those men tonight, without saying anything she took off her gown. She looked just like a little girl about to be bathed by her mother. She quietly walked into the bed side and laid beside me, "what is your name?" asked, Ruth, she said in a real baby tone. How did you get here? I continued, they killed mama and carried me away, she replied, how many men have you slept with since you came here, I asked, without saying a word, she started counting her fingers one, two, three, to ten and she sat up and countered her toes too. She counted eighteen before pausing. Sir, plus you nineteen she said, I shook my head from side to side in dismay, you try and go to sleep, I said, we aren't making love here. Moments later she fell asleep gracefully, I then released and soon slip into a deep sleep myself. The cracking sound of someone trying to gentle open the door to my apartment woke me up. I became determined to stop the practice, I quietly stepped out of my bed and grabbed the stainless cup on the table, and I tip toed to the side of the door and waited patiently. The door swung open slightly and a man's head slowly moved into the room leaving the body outside. When the head was clearly side the apartment, I smashed the stainless cup into the face with all the strength I could muster.

There was a yell and I had the sound of the body drop to the ground, I gently closed the door and tip toed back to the bed, and laid on the girl's body, gently without disturb her peaceful sleep. I remained awake wondering what would happen the next minutes, minute rolled into hours, and yet nothing happened, I soon fell asleep.

For two weeks events of no importance unfolded, no one came to spy on me at night and I had pleaded with the usher to always bring that same girl to me at night. I never messed her up and she soon started calling me daddy because of the fatherly affection I showed her.

I always made sure she's well fed, and I made her as comfortable as possible.

I arrived my apartment very late on 2nd of January 1999 after a hectic schedule, I had accompanied General Mosquito to one of the rebel strong holds from where they hoped to launch an attack on Ecomog's position, I had been shocked by the number of *child soldiers* on that RUF front, in Nigeria, such boys would either be in primary schools, learning one art or hawking their parents wares. But here the are carrying guns that weight close to half of their body weight, killing and are been killed, I just couldn't comprehend with any of the objective of RUF.

When I got to my apartment's entrance, my escorts retreated, I met Ruth sitting on the edge of the bed waiting patiently like a snake that had swallowed a huge prey. ''Daddy!'' She said ''welcome sir, why are you late?'' she embraced me. ''Work! Plenty of work!!'' I explained, I hoped you are alright? Yes Daddy. She said, we sat together at the edge of the bed and we both ate dinner together. She always had the upper hand whenever we ate in the same bowl. Just as most kids, Ruth loved anything food and would do anything to get it, but never thought of exploiting her for once.

After our meal we belched simultaneously triggering some kind of hilarious laughter between us, moment later. I fell asleep, apparently stressed by my day's schedule. Deep into the night, my sleep was halted by Ruth's conversation that started as a murmur, but soon became audible. This night was not the first night Ruth has been involved in mid-night murmuring, I had assumed it to be the normal child's day play reflections in dream. But this night's was with great exception. I became very attentive when my name was mentioned during the discussion. So how did she know my name? I wondered. ''He is a good uncle, he is making me very happy now. I eat plenty food,'' Ruth kept saying several times over.

Goose pimple suddenly covered my skin when I heard the voice of an elderly woman, I pinched my skin quite to make sure I was not in a wild dream land but this is a reality thought. The adult female voice kept consoling Ruth, she said she will follow her where ever she goes and will always protect her, "Ruth!!! I hope you are not asleep," the voice said, today is very important because I want you to follow this uncle in a few days' time, I will make sure he takes you to safety. Always follow him and don't ask questions, because I will be with you, on hearing that statement crystal clear my eyes were forced open, the rebels are planning a full scale invasion of Freetown and I hope to execute my escape during the fighting, how did she know, I thought what my eyes saw made me almost screaming fear. I saw a shadow of a woman on the wall in front of me, I was very sure of everything now. I felt my head enlarging and my heart beat became the only constant rhythm that I could hear clearly. How long have you seen my father and my brother now? Ruth asked, "I see both of them always, but nemesis is chasing your father away from me," the voice replied, "please forgive him mummy," Ruth pleaded,

"I can't, if only we've done that on earth, it would have been alright now, but I can't now, the supernatural omnipotent being controls everything, there I stay, you can do what you are not authorized to do," the voice replied. The scene kept unfolding like a horror movie but I knew I was in contact with reality. Each time the shadow on the wall moved its hand or head in gestures, my fear had no measure. At times I do hold my breath in fear, the voice gave Ruth plenty instructions and each time I closed my eyes and opened it, the shadow remained conspicuous.

I prayed for day break but morning seemed like years away. Suddenly Ruth stopped responding to the voice, "you left me here again, I told you we have to talk till dawn, we still have plenty of things to talk about," the voice complained. I looked at the shadow gesturing, and the shadow stood up abruptly, and slowly moved towards the bed. My eyes began to be water logged as I looked at the shadow stretching its hand over Ruth's face slowly, it started moving towards my head. At that moment I could no longer hold down my fears, I jumped out of bed at the speed of lighting towards the door.

The shadow suddenly vanished and a cat started crying vigorously in the room. I dashed out of the room into the corridor and then, I zoomed off like a rocket propelled man into the jungle, without been spotted by anyone, I crushed tall grasses and tree sprouts, I ran further into the jungle, I suddenly remembered I was putting myself in a grievous danger, so I stopped, without hesitation.

I started joggling back the way I had come. The thought of walking in the jungle bare footed would make the experience totally bearable, great fear, I stared making my way carefully back occasionally my feet picked up tons making the journey both painful and perilous. I took a deep breath when I sighted my apartment from a distance, no one spotted me running out and into the apartment, stood by the door side recuperating from the pain under my foot but the pain began to resurface instead, remain still thinking of how to enter into my apartment, what do I tell people? I thought, I then took the decision not to discuss my ordeal with anyone not even Ruth, when the discomfort of my foot became unbearable I decided to enter my room even if I turned the handle of the room and peeped inside, I saw nothing strange and without hesitation, I sneaked into the room, closed the door gently without clicking the handle to allow for an easy exit if I had to strong out of the room again, Ruth laid motionless on the bed whistling steadily through her nostril as she breathed. My feet ached very badly, I slowly crawled into bed and sleep soon came calling.

The western powers will call such exercise WAR GAME but the rebels call it final assault strategy. It lasted for almost two days. The plot to overrun Freetown was as perfect and as successful, they thought.

I was never given the opportunity to make any contact. In my mind I knew with the combining efforts of the RUF and the military junta, Ecomog's stronghold will crack, I had pleaded with Gen. Mosquito to allow Ruth accompany me to the fronts during the planned attack on Freetown, the first demand to know if I was mad to make such request. But I was relentless on my plea, he finally said, "that's your business," I took that response as an approval of my intention, So I made necessary arrangements for Ruth to come with me, I educated Ruth on what she should do in various occasion and circumstances, I got a military oversized camouflage uniform and a pair of slippers for her, and I carefully cut the sleeve and length of the shirt and trouser to size. With the help of a twine I fasted the trouser to her waist and doubling the twine several times to make buckle for the slippers so it doesn't fall off her feet no matter what happens.

Gen. Mosquito placed me under high surveillance in his convoy, when the D day arrived, I had fifteen rebels tailing me alone, and I had maintained the highest level of calmness ever, as I sat at the back of the Land Rover truck conveying us to the battle front. She didn't ask me any curious question, neither was she curious. The rebels perched on all available spaces on the truck.

We drove through a rough dusty route, I had no idea where the route would land us. Gen. Mosquito rugged four wheel runner jeep cruised behind us, as we drove on the sounds of gun fire and explosions became rife. We drove through thick bushy tracks and bumpy terrains.

The trip made some of the rebels yell in pain occasionally when tree branches and hard shrubs hit them as the vehicles drove on, I didn't say a word as I kept my mind focused on how to play my card very well because any error might cost me my life, I thought what if I should play along and get my first five hundred dollars. What if he didn't pay me, I might never have this opportunity again, and I must take Ruth to safety, and to a new life, my decision to escape became firm.

The vehicles stopped abruptly when it became apparent that the road was no longer accessible and motorable. "Get down," Gen. Mosquito ordered, "it's time we start walk," he said.

Supported by multiple grenade and rocket launchers, along with heavy machine guns and a large entourage. Gen. Mosquito raised his shoulder in a stylish manner as we were led deep into the jungle. The four vehicle convoy was left behind waiting in case the need to escape arise.

I grabbed Ruth by her wrist firmly as we matched deep into the jungle. Ruth didn't complain or ask any curious question but I understand she know more than I did. The dense shrubs would have been unbearable for Ruth but the rebels ahead of us paved the way for us, yet Ruth stumbled occasionally as she half ran and walked to keep up with the pace. "I have conquered all this land area and we are making steady advance," Gen. Mosquito said, suddenly, a phone rang, attracting every one attention I didn't really know a phone was been carried along. Without hesitation, Gen. Mosquito picked the receiver stopping the phone's beeping noise, "Your Excellency, I am aware," Gen. Mosquito said into the phone's mouth piece, "we are pushing steadily. We now have almost all the highway from Lunsar in Port Loko District, to Mile 91, and soon Freetown, will be firmly under our control... oh yes Sir!"

As the conversation progressed, I didn't require a prophet to tell me that a President named Charles from a neighboring country was the Excellency at the other end of the line. "I will keep you updated Your Excellency as we make more progress," General. Mosquito concluded and hung up. One of the rebels was actually assigned to carry the satellite phone on his back.

The faint sound of gun fire and explosion grew louder as we walked further into the jungle. No one spoke except Gen Mosquito, he at times made boastful remarks and issued order gorgeously.

We arrived at an area where a stream flowed across our path. The memory of leeches suddenly gripped my mind. I quickly realized I was better and capable of handling the blood sucking insects this time.

We crossed the stream in one single file. I carried Ruth as we crossed. A few distance away from the stream we met a group of twenty rebels, Gen. Mosquito had a brief discussion with them, his hands pointing to different directions as he spoke in a local dialect. We left the scene afterward and was greeted by the smell of decayed victims of this brutal conflict, and burning substance that could now be felt where we were.

"You can smell my perfume now," Gen. Mosquito said, this is my version of business men perfume, he looked around to acknowledge cheers from his followers, I quickly joined the cheers, by raising my hand above my head, I must use the state house toilet today. Gen Mosquito boasted, just ahead of us are hundreds of combat ready rebels carefully concealing in the bush, An ordinary careless man would step on their toes before realizing it. When it became apparent that we were going to wait there, I whispered to Ruth to sit on the ground. She still looked very strong to me, Gen. Mosquito left us there and walked away further into the bush in company of some rebels.

I became worried that if my strategies and map circling scam should land the rebels in trouble I will never be spared. I prayed and occasionally looked at Ruth. Each time our eyes met I let a stress soaked smile beam to her. A heavy eruption of gun fire made us dive to the nearest bush for cover. I landed with Ruth beside me, I could see the rebels advancing from their position in the distance. Whenever I looked around me I see many eyes staring at me from all angles. I knew it was no time for game playing.

We laid there for about an hour as the fighting raged on heavily, when the intensity of the fighting subsided a little. Gen. Mosquito emerged from the bush, when I saw him, my mind skipped a beat, Reuben, I will promote you very soon, your strategies has given us absolute victory on three important frontlines Gen. Mosquito said with some pride, I forced a smile, that is alright sir, ''more victories will come,'' I replied. He walked up to my side and sat on the ground patting my shoulder. My next target is Lungi, I need that airport badly. Gen. Mosquito said, what can you tell me about the strength in Lungi he said, Lungi is important to me and I know Ecomog's strength in Lungi is over whelming, Gen. Mosquito I said, going to Lungi now will be like hunting in the lion's den, that's where our force are concentrated sorry, I mean Ecomog, that is where they get their supplies from, it is extra ordinarily guarded. We have the man power to break Ecomog's grip the Gen. insisted. A loud explosion interrupted our conversation which made the General almost lay flat on the ground, ''as I was saying,'' he continued, but another blast silenced him again.

When calm finally returned we were ordered to advance, and that the Ecomog's resistance on that front had been crushed and that the rebels were pushing them away rapidly. I got up with Ruth, and carefully followed the advancing rebels who were well ahead of us.

We soon got to an open grass land and later to a major highway; debris littered the high way, trenches had been dug across the high way at several point. We followed the highway amidst echoes of fierce gun battle and explosion. After a while, human casualties of the battle became vivid, mostly women and children, corpses littered the surrounding area, some laid stack naked, mutilated and burnt beyond recognition.

Among the casualties were some Ecomog soldiers whose rifles and belonging had been sized by the rebels. Even a blind goat will know that the rebels were having the upper hand. I pulled Ruth along and she followed gracefully. Some of the rebels that accompanied us were into mopping up operations to clear any pockets of resistance. The steady progress of the rebels bothered me, were the Ecomog troops no longer fighting, I thought? Or has every one suddenly become docile.

Gen. Mosquito had mingled among the rebels so it was very difficult to detect him each time I looked around, eyes were constantly on me, seeking for a false move, but I was determined to wait for the safest occasion to explore; but it seemed never insight. We soon reached the outskirt of Freetown after long hours of horrific sighting and trekking. Most houses that survived the previous hostilities were up in flames, as smoke bellowed into the sky.

We advanced into Freetown, Ruth jerked my hand and pointed to a well, and said she was thirsty, I looked around me and raised my right hand up to attract attention as I moved toward the well with Ruth, a plastic bucket laid beside the well with a long rope attached to it. I picked up the plastic bucket beside the well and moved closer to the side of the well, and peeped into the well, what I saw sent shocks down my spine and it forced my mouth open, the well had been filled with the corpse of mostly little children.

I quickly dropped the bucket and grabbed Ruth by her wrist and hurriedly left the place. My action prompted some of the rebels close to the area to laugh at me. "Uncle," Ruth called, "no water to drink, there is no water in the well. I will get you good water later," I said soothingly. We got to a junction where the look detailed a scene of recent lightly contested battle. More vultures however hovered round that area more than anywhere else. My eyes caught a bullet ridden body of an Ecomog soldier lying beside some barge with a water bottle strapped around his waist, Ruth, please wait here, I said I moved close to the body and untied the water bottle, I shook it and got the feeling it's full. I then opened the bottle and used my shirt to clean round the opening of the bottle, before emptying some of the liquid into my mouth. When I had ascertained it was a drinkable water, I walked over to where Ruth was and handed her the bottle. It took her a few seconds to gulp more than half of the initial content before handing the water bottle back to me. Several rebels had remained still watching my every move. When I looked around, I saw their eyes still on me. I strapped the water bottle around my waist and grabbed Ruth's wrist, and we trailed the rapidly advancing rebels.

A junction forced the rebels to split into three groups and each group followed one of the road that stretched out from the junction. Our group went straight. The split reduced the overwhelming strength of the rebels, so the crushing advance of our group met a stiff resistance along the road from the Ecomog troops. When our advance became stalled with the intensity of the fighting, I and Ruth together with some rebels had to force ourselves into a trench dug across the road for cover, the fighting was getting more intense by the minutes, and considering the level of causality been inflicted on the RUF by the Ecomog Soldiers, the RUF rebels started using civilians as human shield.

Civilians caught up behind the rebel lines became prime target. From where we had sought refuge in the trench, I could see rebels suddenly breaking down doors and forcing out defenseless civilians into the bullet riddled street. Children, women and the elderly were pulled out of their hidings unto the street to act as human shields. The first set of civilians that were forced to the street by the rebels were mauled down by rain of Ecomog bullets. The blood of the innocent children and woman couldn't stop more of them from been pushed into the streets. Within minutes, my eyes became water logged with tears, and I asked myself why God should allow innocent civilians to be so treated. Even beasts do have compassion at times but some humans don't have a trace of remorse, I thought.

I was briefly relieved when Ecomog fire power started declining, and I saw them pulling back. The rebels quickly took advantage of the situation. With civilians as their shield, they heightened their fire power and consolidated their advance while the Ecomog troops were more or less, put on the run, I pulled Ruth out of the trench when it became safe to do so, keeping together off the open space as much as possible, we trailed the advancing RUF rebels, They continued to pull out more civilians out of hiding to the very deadly street using them as human shield.

The battle continued for days and it grew more brutal each day, staying alive became very difficult in the midst of such heightened violence, but somehow, I and Ruth continued to escape with our lives in very unimaginable and dramatic situation.

After days of intense battle, the focus of the fighting gradually shifted to Freetown, the battle for the Sierra Leone Capital intensified with both warring faction deploying everything at their disposal to overcome. But the rebels had better chances because they were better equip than a regional army it was a great surprise.

The RUF rebels were able to over-run the State House in Freetown after an intense resistance by Ecomog troops, Ecomog troops had to withdraw as a result of high civilian casualties and the superior fire power of the rebels; which destroyed parts of the state house.

The absence of Gen. Mosquito was unveiled when I saw a military jeep drive straight to the entrance of the state house, I and Ruth in company of our guards had taken refuge behind a dismantled building during the heated contest for the state house. As General Mosquito stepped out of the jeep, he was quickly surrounded by his body guards, they formed guards of human ring around him.

I shouted out as loud as I could, "General!" Then I saw one of his guards beckoned on me. Without hesitation, I hurried out of my cover. Shots could still be heard but fighting had subsided in front of the state house, corpses of civilians littered the surrounding area. Together with Ruth and my guards we hurried out to meet the General at the entrance of the state house, "Reuben, I told you, I will use the state house's toilet, didn't I?" Gen. Mosquito boasted, "yes, you did" I replied, "Come on let's see how well Ahmed Ka'aba has destroyed Sierra-Leone" Gen Mosquito said,

We all marched into the state house, led by some of the rebels who formed the advance party into the State House. They led us to the top floor and from that height I could see the street below dotted with dead bodies and rebels. "Reuben!" Gen. Mosquito called out, "what do you know about running a government?" He asked. "I don't know how well I understand running a government but, I will find out if I can run one, I replied, I will start forming my government right away, he boasted, One of his aids entered and shouted. "Sir! Sir!! They are on the line" "Good" Gen. Mosquito said, "the world must know," Excuse me and he entered one of the room, looked around and stopped and admired one of the upholstery chair, I sat on one of the chairs with Ruth, then I spotted a refrigerator at a corner. I opened the fridge, it was stocked with fruit juice and wine and beside the fridge I saw packets of biscuit, I brought out a big jug of juice and took some biscuit and came back and sat beside Ruth. She didn't wait for my invitation before pounding on the biscuits as though she has never eaten biscuit before. I had to systematically stuff some of the biscuit into my mouth to match up her pace. She was practically swallowing the biscuits without chewing them. The rebels in the hall soon went for theirs but they stuffed it inside their pockets obviously for the raining day.

When Gen. Mosquito finally came out, we had finished a feast and was only trying to get rid of the biscuit particles clinging between our teeth. I allowed my tongue help me with the cleanup, but Ruth stocked her fingers into her mouth. "What is she eating?" Gen. Mosquito asked, as he settled on an upholstery opposite me, "Oh!" I exclaimed as if I was taken by surprise, "I think she is eating biscuit" I explained, "how could you think she is eating biscuit, while you have been here?" we all kept an expressionless face, "oh no, I just said she's been eating biscuit," I replied, "lumps of biscuits cling to her tooth."

Gen. Mosquito then switched to the main issue. "The international press are at times very stupid. How could some body be asking me about diamond money? What business have they with Sierra-Leonean wealth?" He argued, I listened most of the time during the discussion, only nodding or gesturing when the need arise. He spoke extensively about his murderous and witch-hunting plans.

Later in the day, meal was prepared and we ate together. During the meal, he made a proposal to me to be one of his cabinet ministers, an offer I declined in my mind, but nodded in approval.

I choose to lay on the carpet with Ruth when Gen. Mosquito finally declared bed time, I was flanked by my guards into a large office, Gen. Mosquito had praised my contribution to the RUF rebel movement triumph as the much needed break that enhanced his victory over what he described as West African leaders machines of looters.

I spent the first few hours of the night imagining how it would be like to serve under a blood soaked regime of the RUF, with Corporal Foday as president, I know evil never last for long. My thought, were paused when I felt a shadow move on the wall, the movement suddenly shifted my mind to the ordeal of Ruth and her strange midnight guest, I quickly forced my eyes closed and prayed that that event shouldn't repeat itself here, I know if I dare run anywhere I will be shot, considering the level of the rebel's alertness in the State House. Ruth's tiny body laid just a few inches away from mine. I could tell she was fast asleep as she laid motionless with her mouth wide open and saliva trickling out, time crawled on without anything eventful puncturing the relentless melodies of insects.

I woke up when my skin was dampened by a liquid, I slowly sat up, I turned and examined the liquid, it turned out to be Ruth's urine, it had flowed to my chest and was heading for my chin when I woke up, I hissed in disgust and moved out of the way of the spreading urine.

I took my bath that morning and rinsed my clothing I had instructed her to wash her dress and put them on wet, as punishment for her action.

Gen. Mosquito called a conference of some of his Commanders and Aides that morning, most of the issues discussed were all self-centered issues, how to share power and wealth were the songs on their lips. My mind was filled with hate for the so called liberator, I was soon convinced beyond reasonable doubt that their intensions were purely centered around accumulation of wealth, I prayed in my mind for their plans to be dashed before a call came in midway during the conference.

Gen. Mosquito went to the corner of the hall where his satellite phone was temporarily installed to receive the call from the distance I over heard him say "your Excellency!" each time he spoke, coupled with other things he said, it became clear that the conversation had been with President Charles of a neighboring country.

After the call Gen. Mosquito assigned me to flip through heaps of files and document, I neither knew nothing about or their origin. The act was so boring that I openly hissed occasionally to express my disgust but I got very busy with it whenever Gen. Mosquito came around to see how I was doing. I satisfied his curiosity, expressing opinion where necessary irrespective of the fact that I knew next to nothing about them.

Before retiring to sleep that night Gen. Mosquito had expressed his worries over a report of a crushing defeat his rebels suffered on a front and a voice of American radio reported that Ecomog was expecting reinforcement from Nigeria and Ghana. The assurance he got from President Charles of getting more mercenary from Liberia to sharpen his defense, gave him some reasons to brightened up. It occurred to me after several days to say a short prayer before lying down that night, I took severe action against Ruth to prevent a reoccurrence of what happened the previous night, I laid her by my side on the floor with the intention of flogging her the next morning if she ever wet the floor again. "Sorry Daddy, I will not wee-wee here again," she promised after my serious warning.

I slept gracefully that night for the first time since my entry into the State House until a loud explosion jerked every one out of sleeping. More explosion were heard accompanied by outburst of machine gun fire I always slept with my clothing on, which made it pretty easy form to dress up. As Ruth saw me lacing my boot in a haste she also scrambled for her jacket and slippers in confusion, she wanted to wear both simultaneously, I quickly intervened by collecting the jacket. So she hurriedly put on her slippers, I handed back the jacket to her which she hurried put on. Confusion had engulfed everywhere and the number of guards detailed to me had reduce to two by the time I finished helping Ruth dress up, I crawled to a nearby window overlooking the side view of the State House. I could only see sparks of light and hear sounds of explosion in the distance, I crawled back to where Ruth was, looking like a terrified rat, we both sat on the floor while my two guards occasional poked their head out to fire shots aimlessly. The urge to escape suddenly gripped my mind, I knew Ecomog troops were determined to dislodge the rebels from the State House. If the State House should suddenly fall to the hands of Ecomog troops my Freedom would be achieved.

The only source of light that illuminated the entire town was the bright night stars and the occasionally spark from the distant blast. The battle line began to diminish from the initial two kilometers or there about to less than a kilometer to the State House.

At that point Gen. Mosquito didn't need a referee to blow a withdrawal whistle for him and his rebels. We suddenly heard the voice of The General barking out orders. "All the guards out, I want you all out here, only the combatants should remain," he ordered, two guards on hearing the order suddenly turned their gun towards me and Ruth, Ruth's eyes glittered in the darkness as we looked into each other's eyes. Move outside one of the guards ordered hastily. I felt it's very foolish to play smart but it's wise to play foolish in front of a loaded gun, so I quietly stood up and together with Ruth we came out to the open office where Gen. Mosquito stood. "Ha, Rueben!" He shouted, when he saw me, come out to the open we have to make a tactical retreat immediately, he said, "it's okay Sir," I replied, "we are using the left exit, so move, move, move," he urged.

I grabbed Ruth by her wrist and together we ran alongside some of his aids who led us to the exit, many loots had already been jammed packed into the four vehicles that were packed outside, and their engines running in readiness. We stood by the side of one of the jeep under the watchful eyes of the gun tooting guards listening to sporadic gun ire and explosions that became louder each time. More loots were still been hauled into any available space in the vehicles by the rebels.

When Gen. Mosquito emerged from the building, the vehicles had been stuffed to the brims, with lots of computers, T.V. Sets, small generating sets, files, foods, drinks, small furniture etc.

"Let's go, let's go" Gen Mosquito ordered, I helped Ruth climb onto the back of one of the waiting vehicle and I immediately joined her. Our vehicle led the way out of the State House and other vehicles followed behind. The vehicle wheels screamed as we dashed to the highway in frightening speed, I had no idea where the vehicles were heading but as we left the state house the fighting began to fade gradually into the distant behind us.

Soon the State House vanished completely from my sight and I could only hear the distant blast of explosions and gun fire. The flash of lightings continued to diminish gradually, due to the jam packed cargo in the vehicle, we had very few space to squeeze ourselves in, thus making the trip less comfortable. We soon zoomed past all structures littering the road side. Just a few of them still had resemblance of what they used to looked like, while most of them had been turned into hip of debris by explosion.

We drove far into the jungle along the path way that led the way to next stronghold of the RUF. I closed my eyes and prayed briefly thanking God for all he has done for me so far and I requested for more favors. By the time I was through with my meditation, Ruth had started nodding her head from side to side in a state of slumber, I looked at her sharply. Children don't worries much I thought, suddenly, there was an outburst of compressed air, and the loud noise triggered some level of panic amongst us. "Tyre!" the driver shouted in disgust, the action of the driver quickly reduced our panic, as he carefully stirred the vehicle to a halt, the three other vehicles in the convoy also pulled off the main road close to ours.

Our driver was the first person to get off the vehicle. I woke Ruth up and I helped her out of the vehicle. "What is the problem" Ruth demanded, I told her we had a flat tyre and that we were trying to fix it. The voice of Gen. Mosquito made every one turn to his direction, "you are a stupid man, how can you run into this mess," he asked in anger, the driver didn't alter a word, but hurriedly went about the process of changing the faulty tyre which incidentally was the one on his side.

One of the rebels assisted in fixing the jack. As the jack began lifting the vehicle's front axle gradually, the jeep then drifted due to the slippery level of the road, "get a wedge quickly," the driver yelled. We quickly looked around for stone or object that could serve as a wedge for the sliding vehicle. It was during the wedge searching expedition I observed that the rebels' attention were not on me, and Gen. Mosquito had retired into his jeep packed in the middle of the convoy. I hurriedly went to where Ruth stood, she placed her left foot on a stone. "Get aside" I ordered and I lifted the oval shaped stone off the ground to the drifting jeep, I quickly used the stone to wedge the back wheel, and exhale a breath of relief, feeling proud to have prevented the jeep from rolling off the jack completely.

I then thought of exploring this great opportunity. "Ruth come and drink the water you demanded for," I said, in an effort to attract Ruth to where I was standing, all the rebels that went to hunt for wedges for the jeep soon arrived and converged round the faulty vehicle, and few of the rebels took strategic positions around the areas, I gave Ruth a pat on her back and quickly whispered a few instructions into her ear, telling her to get ready to run after me as fast as she could.

I grabbed her left arm tightly and we sluggishly walked to the side of the faulty jeep and stood very close to where I had placed the wedge behind the rear tyre. I looked around sharply to be sure no one was watching and carefully observed as the faulty tyre was successfully detached from the axle leaving only the jack to support the weight of the vehicle on that side. I quickly but firmly kicked off the wedge supporting the vehicle and the jeep slipped off the jack supporting it. That incident sparked off confusion as the rebels allied round the jeep to lift it up again. Gen. Mosquito only laughed briefly, as he stayed put in his jeep.

Within a split of second, I pulled Ruth with me as I dashed into the bush, I ran as fast and as carefully as I could so I didn't drag Ruth to the ground. I was amazed by her speed as we both crashed through hard shrubs heading further into the jungle, I guessed lifting up the jeep had occupied the minds of the rebels more than I ever thought before taking the risk. We ran deep into the jungle for about three minutes before we over heard the rebels call out our names. My heart skipped a beat, I knew they will soon be after us, I broke off several thick branches from thick shrubs as we dashed further into the jungle, I heard a voice say, "look for them, look for them," a voice I recognized to be that of Gen. Mosquito. We had no idea where we were heading into the darkness. The head lamp of one of the jeep flashed deep into the jungle ahead of us. We hurried stayed away from the light ray.

From the distance we were still able to hear the rebels behind us. Each time it seemed their voices were getting louder, if I'm ever caught, I thought, I knew the deadly consequences that await me, being part of the rebels is no pride to a worthy citizen of any nation. I felt I did what was right.

Later I had a voice say "No sign of them" Spray the bush with bullets, another voice ordered, I recognized to be that of Gen. Mosquito, then an out bust of machine gun fire rented the night's silence, like an aggressive bull I dragged Ruth to the ground. We both landed on a sharp body pricking shrubs and remained still as the rebels sprayed the jungle with bullets.

Several minutes later the shooting died down. As the shots seized, I heard Ruth call "Daddy! I am afraid," "don't worry I will take you home," I assured her, I patted her shoulder gently.

The night's tensed silence permitted us to hear the jeeps engine roar to life and soon started fading away gradually. I was not sure if all the vehicles had been driven off. I stood up slowly looking round me for any strange movement but here was none. "Get up," I ordered "we must get away from here now," I said quietly.

We wondered deep into the jungle. Ruth accidentally entangled her feet in a shrub, she stumbled and fell. I then decided to allow Ruth rest where she sat on the ground, whistling out of her nostrils, I started thinking of how we could pass the remaining part of the night here, I carefully leveled the shrubs around where she laid with my feet in a square shape of about seven feet apart. By the time I was through with the task, Ruth's breath had normalized and she sat up. "What are you going to do here," she asked, pointing to the center of the leveled area. We are sleeping here tonight I answered, I sat right at the center of the leveled area looking up into the night sky as if I had the assignment to count the distant stars.

Ruth came close to my side and touched my shoulder, "how do we go home," she asked, "that is what am trying to find out," I said, not looking towards her, we sat on the ground together in silence listening to the insects melodious calls and feeling the wind's whistling sound. Ruth, soon began to slumber, nodding her head back and forth, I watched her briefly and almost busted out laughing, I eased her back, gently to the ground with my right hand. She hesitated and allowed me rest her back on the ground. In no time, she was fast asleep and I was left alone to behold the night. I used the relative calm around me to say my prayer to God, I had no weapon of any sort to counter any attack but I had a feeling of security.

I found myself dosing off gradually, and before long, I opted to lay on my back to continue my supplication, as I did so my gaze was fixed into the night sky and I felt I was looking into God's eye I silently said my prayers. My comfortable posture soon made me slip into a deep sleep.

The cry of a night bird interrupted my sleep and my eye was immediately forced closed when I opened it, I saw the same figure of the other nigh sitting close to Ruth and the woman like creature was busy plaiting Ruth's hair, the way a mother waves her little stubborn daughter's hair. I slowly opened my eyes each time to look at this creature, the thought of taking to my heels didn't cross my mind, and I laid on the ground motionless and prayed within me for an end to this horrific episode unfolding before my eyes.

My entire body was enveloped by goose pimples and I felt my head expand each time I dared to look at the creature but she looked deeply involved with the weaving of Ruth's hair, I remained terrified and curious about this strange creature. Its second appearance casted no doubt about the reality of this being. The cries of nocturnal birds grew louder each time putting more freight into my already petrified mind. My eyes could neither stay close nor open.

When the creature was done with Ruth's hair, it slowly stood up, and stared at Ruth for some time before it turned towards my directions, and for the first time my eyes came in contact with it eyes the glittering greenish eye that caught mine and it put more than fear into me. Jesus!! Gushed out of my mouth uncontrollable, I felt the weight of an elephant on my entire body. I tried to raise my hand, not even one of my fingers responded to my intension. The only thing I could manage do with serious difficulty then was to call the name of Jesus, the name kept pouring out of my mouth with difficulty, but I was not sure if anyone else heard me but I knew my God was by my side and to my rescue.

Suddenly, the creature started vanishing in bits, the legs first became invisible leaving the upper body suspended and the greenish eye glittering, which appeared to be penetrating into mine. Then the upper body followed, leaving the head dangling in space, when the head finally disappeared, I felt myself been propelled to my feet by a weird force, I stood in confusion, not knowing which direction to run to, despite the cold night breeze my entire body was soaked in my sweat, in my confused state of mind, I resolved to sit on the ground away from where Ruth laid, with breath wrestling out of her nostrils she appeared ignorant, with my head bowed. I prayed in silence for an end to this inexplicable encounter with the strange creature, I prayed until dawn without disturbing Ruth.

Ruth's good morning interrupted my prayer. My eyes went straight to her hair, I saw no sign of any weaving on her hair, I then looked all over her, I saw no difference from what she used to look like but a section of her trouser looked damp and immediately knew she had wet herself with her urine, I looked straight into her eyes and she appeared to be ignorant of what had earlier happened, and I wondered if she was trying to pretend, I felt very confident confronting her because I knew I had no evil in mind for her, "Ruth! come here," I called out pointing to a big stone beside me. The sound of insects had subsided for songs from boringly coloured birds that seemed to have taken over all three tops around us.

When she finally settled down on the big stone beside me, I started softly, "Ruth, you are a small girl, I never want to bother your mind about this matter but I can no longer remain silent while I suffer within me," she looked confused as I spoke in riddles, "please, I beg you, tell me about your unusual night friend," She hesitated, "I don't have any friend you are my only friend," she answered, I suddenly realized it was no time for fact finding talk getting to a safe place was more essential now. So I quickly summed up the issue telling her that she should think about the question properly before giving me an answer.

"Ruth, trying to be optimistic. We have to look for a way to my camp where my friends are. We will be safe there," I said, "when are we going to reach your camp," she asked, "I will tell you when I find the way," I answered.

We started out that morning. Without knowing the actual direction to go, but we kept heading deeper into the jungle. By sunrise we had covered several kilometers deep into the jungle, when I spotted a mango tree covered with its own ripe fruits. I drew Ruth's attention to the tree, "let's go and eat some mango" She urged, "I don't need a prophet to tell me that," I replied.

I approached the base of the mango tree with caution, with Ruth behind. Due to the presence of over ripe fruits on the ground, I thought it could well be a good place for snakes to breed, and to also feed on insect and maggot. Some few meters away from the feet of the tree my thoughts was confirmed when I spotted a python of about five feet long running its tongue over a ripe mango fruit on the ground, I hesitated, abruptly, and Ruth crashed unto my back suddenly, "Sorry! Sorry!!" She said, "shhh! Don't move, snake," I warned.

Without looking at Ruth I carefully looked around for a stick, the entire surrounding was covered by dense shrub. When my search for a stick failed, I decided to use unripe mango fruits as stone. I moved slowly to the side of the mango tree where it branch was closer to the ground due to the weight of the unripe bunches of fruits.

I kept my eyes fixed as often as possible on the snake which looked motionless except for its flicking tongue around the mango fruit. The first fruit I casted at the snake land some few centimeters away from the snake's head, the snake moved it head reluctantly away from the mango fruits. The second unripe fruit threw caught it midsection, and the impact made the reptile to act in self-defense, its movement became even more swift. It moved closer to the base of the mango tree and started climbing the tree faster than I thought it could move. My third missile brought the snake back to the ground, it swung swiftly and faced Ruth where she stood watching. As it dashed towards Ruth she turned and ran the opposite direction.

I threw several unripe fruits at the moving snake and no one struck it. Moving away from my position will deny me access to the unripe fruits, so I maintained my position and kept aiming my target. I was forced to abandon my position by the snake's aggression towards Ruth, she turned and ran for a brief distance before she stumbled and fell to the ground, the snake charged towards her aggressively without hesitation, in fear and confusion, I ran after the snake, seeing Ruth helpless on the ground with the snake a few inches away from her. I dashed toward it and grabbed the tail of the snake with the speed of lightening and threw it several meters away, I heard it body land with a thud.

I quickly pulled Ruth to her feet and we ran the other way, I slowed Ruth down when I was sure we've ran several hundred meters away from the snake. We both shivered in fear as we looked at each other. I pulled her to myself and held her, I felt her heart beating rapidly, pounding my chest. "Sorry Ruth, it will be alright," I said, her warm tears suddenly started wetting my chest as she sobbed uncontrollably. I pat her back to console her. It took me several minutes before I could console her.

When I finally did, I tried to tease her, "I will like you to follow me to Nigeria," I asked, "I will always follow you to anywhere," she answered in her tears logged eyes.

We continued our journey through the dense shrubs. I led the way parting the dense shrub with both hands. We really said nothing to each other, except when I had to warn her of something. "Monkey! Monkey!!" Ruth shouted suddenly, I asked in confusion I can hear monkeys talking, listen, she said I exhaled in relief, I thought the monkeys were very close to us, I listened and heard noise in the far distance. I have never encountered herds of monkeys in my life, and I never anticipated it. I reached for a nearby tender stem, broke it off its base, and stripped it of its greenish leaves, I carried the stick with me as we tore through the jungle. The noise of the monkeys grew louder as we made our way further into the jungle.

By the time we got to a section of the jungle with blooming flower plant, the sounds of the monkey had subsided, and with the help of my stick I plugged plenty of palm fruits from a palm tree and we hungrily chewed the fruits.

After a while, as we sat eating the fruits at the bottom of the palm tree, Ruth started throwing up after eating much of the palm fruits. I knew she was exhausted, so I allowed her to lay on the grass. Within minutes she fell asleep. When I became sick of chewing the palm fruit, I stretched my body and laid on the grass beside Ruth, and I also feel asleep afterward.

When I woke up I was greeted by a humming sound, I quickly sat up and looked to the direction of the sound, what I saw stunned me, the biggest untamed monkey I have ever seen sat a few meters away chewing palm fruits, I ran my right hand over my face to be sure I wasn't in a trance, I heard several other of such sounds, looking round me, I saw that we have been surrounded by a herd of palm fruits chewing monkeys, they comprised of various age groups, the parents and children. When the biggest of all the monkey saw that I had sat up, it made an aggressive charge toward me then hesitated, he tried to scare me away. Ruth remained in her sleep when the frequency of the aggression of the biggest monkey towards me became unbearable, I decided to react. I know I could never run away leaving Ruth behind. So I decided to battle the monkeys.

The next aggressive move of the monkey met my resistance. I swung the stick was holding very violently at the charging monkey and struck the monkey on its neck, and caused her to cry out in pain which attracted the other monkeys that had been busy eating palm fruit. They have been paying less attention to our encounters. I became even more mentally destabilized when I noticed that almost all the monkeys had taken a violent turn towards me, all the monkeys encircled I and Ruth, Ruth was still asleep and gradually the tightened the cycle around us. Not knowing which direction to strike with my stick, I became confused, the monkey were closing their circle slowly to a few feet away from us when Ruth suddenly woke up, their persistent cries must have woken her up, Ruth became fully aware of the danger we were facing and she screamed so loud in an unbelievable manner that could penetrate the ear of a deaf person.

Her scream made the monkeys stop abruptly and the biggest of all the monkey hesitated briefly then turned and ran off followed by the other monkeys. Without hesitation I pulled Ruth to her feet and we both ran towards the opposite direction.

The sun was high and intense. And the air was still but filled with the aroma of chlorophyll of the green vegetation.

We slowed down several minutes' later breathing heavily out of exhaustion. We looked at each other thoughtfully, with sweat streaming out of our skin. We looked like athletes on the finish line of a sprint. When I became fully conscious of where we stood. I saw we were in the midst of a plantation, the entire field was filled with plant of similar height and nature, I bent over and examined the plants carefully and my mind felt we must have stumbled on an India hemp field. "What is this" Ruth asked? I held my two fingers out and brought it close to my lips. "Cigarette?" she asked, "yes, bad cigarette," I replied, without venturing deep into the field we kept to the side of the plantation then suddenly a voice shouted, "hold it there!" I froze in fear, and Ruth quickly clung to my left arm in fear. I slowly raised my stick up and turned to see who the owner of the voice was, "don't turn, stay as you are, the voice ordered.

I quietly obeyed. A fearsome bearded man in his late thirties, dark in complexion, and with a bald head carrying an AK47 assault rifle pointed straight at me. My left hand on Ruth's breast felt the rapid vibration of her heart beat.

"what do you want here" the man asked? "am sorry we've trespassed on your property, we are lost in the jungle and somehow we wander here," I said confidently, trying to conceal my fears.

"Drop your weapons," the man ordered, "No weapon sir," I replied. "No weapon?" The man asked, "my friend your stick!" he ordered. I quickly allowed my stick drop to the ground, striking my feet in the process. He stepped closer to me and kicked the stick further away from my reach. little girl, leave his hand, he ordered, before Ruth could react to the order I quickly pulled my hand out of her hold brushing my hand against her breast and face in the process, am Sorry Ruth, I apologize, my hand pointed straight up into the sky, "search him," the man ordered, I wondered who was to search me. But to my surprise a second man jumped down from the top of a nearby mango tree.

He was a lanky bearded man, looking much younger than the first. He wore a tee shirt with the inscription NOTHING GOES FOR NOTHING, His black trouser was torn from the side revealing his tiny hairy leg. He also carried an assault rifle. His blood shot eyes scared me, his boney left hand ran over my entire body, when he got to my pubic area he trusted his hand aggressively in and out, the pain forcing me to swing a knock-out punch at the man's jaw as my punch caught its target, a force stroke me from behind my head and I became unconscious.

I regained consciousness in a wooden/muddy hut, my hands and legs were tied apart to four separate iron pegs on the floor. I tried to struggle free but the ropes proved tougher. I laid helplessly, staring into the tattered roof of the hut. My mind drifted to what happened between I, Ruth and those monkeys, the monkeys are animals, but they felt for one another, they reacted to the plight of each other and they came to the rescue of one of theirs. But humans are instead inflicting pains, hardships and sorrow on their fellow brothers, despite being the most advance and clever of all animals.

For a moment, I suddenly wished God had made me one of those monkeys. I became very worried when I couldn't see any sign of Ruth around me, what has those bastard done to her? I wondered, "Ruth!!!" I shouted as loud as I could, but the door of the hut suddenly swung open and two boys both carrying a rifle walked into the hut, and pointed their rifle at me. "Mr. Man, what is your problem?" one of them demanded, I remained silent and felt frightened by the look of the boys, "do you know you are disturbing our president, the other boy said and walked straight to the side of my head and lifted his left leg without removing his boots, "open your mouth." He ordered, I hesitated. "I say open your wide mouth or I will cut off your ear," he threatened. The other boy pulled out a knife from the side of his right boot and smiled, I hurriedly complied and opened my mouth, he trusted his boot into my mouth trying to force it deeper down my throat, the other boy laughed as groaned in pain and disgust, he inflicted the pain for several minute, when he was satisfied with his action, he then pulled out his boot from month. I felt like my mouth had being torn apart by a wild beast.

"I want to drive my car," the other boy said, as he walked up between my separated legs and placed one of his feet on my testicles and gently used his feet to transfer some of his body weight onto my testicles, sending a devastating sharp pain to my brain, I yelled in pain, "shut up my friend," his partner snapped, when I couldn't stop crying he trusted his feet deep into my mouth, I had the feeling that the end had come for me that moment, the pain was excruciating.

They both laughed as I cried out in pain, and in my mind I prayed to God to come to my rescue as that was the only weapon I had, I became exhausted, no strength left in me. Then suddenly, a machine gun fire erupted outside the hut and, in a second, bullets spilled into the hut striking the boys all over their body. They were huddled together by the bullet and slammed to the ground.

The pains I felt continued for several seconds as if it was still been inflicted on me. When my wailing stopped, the shot sized, I gasped for breath as I saw Ruth dash into the hut carrying an automatic rifle that seemed very heavy for her to carry, her nakedness was only covered by the pant she wore, she ran to my side, and laid the gun down, and quickly dragged one of the boy, whose body lay across my stomach off, and picked up the boys knife, within seconds she succeeded in cutting off all the ropes that bounded me to the ground.

When I was able to sit up I spat repeatedly before picking up the gun, "take off his jacket and wear it quickly," I ordered I went close to the door and peeped as I saw no one coming, but only a lifeless body laid on the ground, I rushed inside the hut and assisted Ruth remove and wear one of the boys jacket, I peeped again until we became sure no one was insight, I held Ruth's wrist with my left hand and the machine gun with my other hand as we ran into the surrounding bush.

After we had covered several distance, I decided we stop running and instead walk. The sun had vanished from the sky and birds were busy heading for their nests. I carefully led the way to an unknown destination as some of the pain within me eased and gave way gradually. My attention was attracted by some ripe mango fruits I stepped on. "Maggot! I shouted," I quickly picked up one and gave it to Ruth and helped myself with another one. I munched the fruit hungrily. We continued eating the fruit one after the other as I sat at the feet of the mango tree without saying much to Ruth, the thought of the risk of a running stomach prevented me from eating even more of the fruits but I stuffed a couple of the fruits into my pocket. When I stood up, I stretched and belched in the process. I was not putting on any shoe, I looked around, wondering if I had remove them recently, I later became convinced I didn't run into the jungle with my boot on, when I didn't see anything like shoe around. I became curious, I then noticed that Ruth was bare footed, our shoe had been taken off earlier.

As darkness crawled in gradually. I began to feel the absence of my shoe and occasionally we step on piercing plants and it hurt badly. It soon became too dark for us to continue wandering in the jungle, so I decided we pass the night under an umbrella like tree. "Ruth, you sleep here," I said, pointing to where I had neatly laid pawpaw leaves on the ground. The bright night sky provided us with enough light to recognize even ant, and night birds orchestra provided the much needed melodies of nature.

I sat down with my back against a nearby tree and examined the machine gun to see if there was any need for an adjustment, I found out the gun was in order. I laid it on my laps and relaxed. "Ruth, how did you get this gun?" I asked, "the man wants to force me, I carried his gun and fired him, and I had yours voice screaming, I came there and fired those boys," she said, "if I had been standing I would have been killed by your shootings" I said, "I peeped into the hut before shooting," she replied. "who thought you how to shoot?", I asked? "The RUF thought me how to shot and I see people shoot always", she replied, her eyes balls glittering in the dim skylight, and it suddenly reminded me of our night companion, I prayed silently, "Lord, unto thy hand I committee my spirit now and always," I thought I should go elsewhere to sleep as soon as she is asleep.

"Ruth, I owe you a lot, when I get you home, I shall pay a lot," I said, moving her aside, I spoke to her softly until she fell asleep. When I became convinced she was deeply in asleep, I left her side to the base of a tree which was about fifty meters away, but she was still within my sight.

I hid the gun down beside me and made the area ready for a little comfort. When I was satisfied with the layout, I laid down with the machine gun on my right side, I kept my eye fixed on Ruth to be sure nothing disturb her peaceful sleep. If that creature appears tonight, I would be in a safe distance not to feel its presence, after this recent incident in which Ruth played a very vital role in our escape, I became more committed and affectionate to her situation.

I tried very hard to fall asleep but to no avail, the night peace was interrupted late into the night when the wind blew violently rocking trees and shrubs back and forth, I cursed and got up and gripped the gun and ran to Ruth's side soon it started raining. I laid my gun down and went for more pawpaw leaves which I carefully laid on Ruth's body to protect her from the dropping rain. The sound of thunder and lightning kept frightening me, I gathered the remaining pawpaw leaves and headed for my initial spot. I was only a few meters away from Ruth. When I saw a white creature appear and she sat where I had been a while ago before the storm started. My entire body was covered with gross pimples and my head swell in fear. A loud thunder and lightning made me drop the gun quietly, without picking up the gun, I ran back to Ruth and laid beside her, and buried my head under a leaf where I laid shivering. Not again my God, I thought, I dared not to look at the white robed creatures that sat motionless staring at me. I knew deep in my heart that I meant no harm to its interest, so I can't be hurt, I thought, but its appearance would scare even the greatest warrior to his marrow.

In the most unusual twist of event I fell into a deep sleep seconds after my encounter, unlike before I had no idea of what transpired afterward until the next morning.

I woke up the next morning quite late when the ray of the sun beamed across my face, Ruth had got up much earlier feasting on ripe mango fruits. The dews on leaves reminded me that it rained the previous night. I examined my whole body, I looked quit dry down to my pants. I wondered, what would have kept me dry under the rain without any adequate shelter, "Ruth!" I called, "good morning Daddy," she answered, in a rather strong and unusually Sierra-Leonean accent, "come here quickly," I ordered. When she got to my side, I pulled her closer and felt her clothing, she was also dry to my surprise, beside her wet feet and mango juice smeared hands. I was left wondering what really happened yester night.

I picked up the machine gun, examined it thoroughly and found nothing wrong with the rifle. It remained loaded. "We have to leave here immediately," I ordered. As we foraged through the dense shrubs, my mind dabbled over what led to my strange experience the previous night, I knew God was solidly behind me. Even when I am faced with tribulations and uncertainty.

Getting around in the jungle barefooted is not a pleasant experience at all, thorns, dried sticks and sharp weeds always reminds us that we were bare footed, whenever we mistakenly stepped on them. The pain forced Ruth to shed tears on several occasions. Aside from the pain under our foot, the birds entertained us with hilarious melodious tune. By sun rise, we had wandered very far into the jungle, despite our handicap.

"Look over there Daddy, I like that small beautiful rabbit," Ruth said, pointing to a rabbit beside a small tree. The rabbit had a mixture of white and brown furs covering all of its body. Except its big dark eyes that rotted from side to side, the beauty of the little animal also fascinated me to the extent that I was tempted to catch the animal alive, what should I do with this little innocent animal I thought briefly. Finding nothing important, I decided I would let the animal go. When I ignored Ruth's request, "please Daddy, I love to carry the rabbit," she pleaded, looking exhausted, "you don't need the rabbit, it's dangerous," I said, trying to persuade her to forget about the rabbit but she insisted when tears started rolling down her cheek, the desire to keep her happy always griped my mind and for a brief moment I stood motionless. "Hold this carefully," I said handing the rifle over to her.

I slowly turned and faced the rabbit, it started to run in my direction blindly, what an innocent peaceful animal it was, I moved closer gradually on my knee in an attempt to catch it, it made no attempt to escape, I thought it would be an easy catch for me. So, I turned and motioned Ruth to come join me trap the rabbit, she decided to go down on her knees while holding on to the rifle. I kept crawling until I was some few feet away from the Rabbit, suddenly my right hand touched something buried inside the ground, and in a split second what I touched triggered a booby trap.

A very large truck of wood fitted with sharp metal blade swung dangerously from the top of a tree toward us. I quickly dived side way and grabbed Ruth, I rolled over with Ruth in the process. Before the trap could reach us, we had rolled out of it path. It landed with a huge force and it dragged on, one of its sharp metal blade pierced the rabbit, dragging it along in the process. I laid on the ground motionless imagining what would have happened to us, I carefully stood up and picked up the rifle with my right hand. "Ruth! Up, let's go," I ordered, as we left the scene, tears streamed out of Ruth's eye uncontrollably.

After walking for several hours in the jungle, we decided to rest under an umbrella shaped tree. We waited patiently till dusk, when the sun was below the horizon, Ruth had slept and woken up several times over when I suddenly heard whistling that sounded like a bird but I suspected it was not from any living bird, so I intensified my surveillance quietly on every corner of the plantation for any human presence.

Several minutes later my surveillance paid off, when a young man in his early twenties dressed in a yellow short sleeve shirt and black trouser was spotted on the scene. He had his hair shaved clean, reminding me of the main actor of Kojak, a popular American movie series, he stepped out beneath a dense undergrowth at the edge of the hemp plantation.

"I would never have detected a mouse there," Ruth whispered, "shut up," I snapped, I watched the man cross into the plantation. Minutes later, he came out with a sack on his head, he crossed into the plantation again, "can you, make it across today?" A voice asked, "why, sure," the young man answered excitedly.

The second man then jumped down from the top of a tree at the edge of the plantation. I wondered if he had spotted us, however, his actions assured me we've not been spotted. The second man had no shirt on but his faded blue jeans trouser seemed oversized. He too was clean shaved but looked well built from his waist upward and carried an automatic rifle cross his shoulder in a manner the Fulani herds men in Northern Nigeria carry their stick. The two men stood and whispered for minutes, the way they gestured, I felt they were perfecting a strategy, my mind skipped a beat when the two men suddenly abandoned their discussion and started walking towards our direction, I quickly and quietly released the safety catch of my rifle, and my heart pumped harder as the two men approached us slowly. When they were about seventy meters away, a third man came out of his hideout with his rifle further compounding my fears, but I managed to put on a tough mood, as the men approached Ruth she tighten her grip on my feet in fear.

They pass by our hideout without noticing our presence, when they were some distant away from us. I yelled, "don't move or I rip you open," The men immediately remained still, I carefully walked out of my hiding with my rifle pointing in my hand steadily pointing at the men. Don't move, I barked, repeatedly one of the men attempt looking back, Throw your weapons into the bush, I ordered, two of the men on my right immediately complied but the third man who had no shirt on played a fast trick that almost cost my life, in a split of a second he stretched his right hand with his gun out as if he wanted to drop his gun, but he quickly swung round with his gun to fire at me.

I quickly intercepted his smart move by smashing my rifle straight into his face before he could complete his deadly swing. It caught him on the fore-head cracking his skull terribly, and he fell with his face to the ground after hesitating for a few seconds. My swift counter action stunned the other two men who immediately took to their heels. I quickly squeezed the trigger of my gun spilling several bullets above the heads of the fleeing men, and accompanied by my stop order, the two men immediately stopped, "if you dare move an inch I will blow you apart, Ruth!, come here, pick up their guns," I ordered.

She came out shivering, when she had finished picking up all the rifles, the third man on the ground rolled over then staggered to his feet with a bloody face. "Sit on the ground now," I shouted. The three men quickly complied with my order. The steady stream of blood from the head of the third man told me he will soon be out of blood if nothing is done to help him. "Who are you?" I asked, "we are farmers," one of the men answered in a shaky and husky voice, "farming weeds and weapons for The RUF, right!" I asked, "keep quiet, you all belong to the RUF," I continued, "NO," they yelled in chorus, "we are farmers and we sell our products across the border," one of the men interrupted, pointing backward, "you are all lying, you all belong to the RUF," I insisted, "it's not right," the three men said in a chorus, Ruth had successfully arranged the two rifles on her head carrying them like a bunch of fire wood, I studied the three men thoughtfully, "who is your leader?" I asked, they looked at each other briskly before the one in his pool of blood answered, "I am the leader," raising his left hand up while he held the other hand firmly against his bloody fore head, perhaps, to curb the persistent bleeding, "what is your name," I asked? "Spencer," he answered and pointing the barrel of my gun at the men one after the other, "George, Frank," they all answered one after the other, I realized I needed their assistance to find my way easily to join my Ecomog colleagues. "You Frank help your boss stop his bleeding," I ordered, "and no funny tricks, else you will be sorry," I warned, he slowly dipped his unsteady right hand inside a sack he had earlier dropped on the ground and brought out a small bottle containing a substance. He took off his shirt and used it to apply the substance in the bottle to Spencer's bleeding fore-head and he gently held the shirt against his forehead,

I kept a close watch on the men for any false move, A few minutes later Spencer's bleeding stopped. "Alright, take me to your base," I snapped, the men reluctantly led the way through a path. I gave them about two meter distance before allowing Ruth to follow suite with the rifle on her head, "for no reason should any of you look back, except I asked you to do so," I warned, sounding very tough to the three men.

I carefully used the calm situation to unload the men's rifle Ruth carried on her head one after the other. With my left hand and a little support from my right hand, I did it so perfectly none of the men got a tip of it. When I had succeeded in securing the bullets inside my trouser pockets I hurriedly gave Ruth a pat on the back.

Each time the hard shrubs would brush our face as we tried to find our path. After disrupting the peace of several tiny colourful birds, we arrived a place in the depth of the jungle, I spotted four huts with tattered roofs and wooden partition, and the huts were suspended on a wooden raft with rooms for loads beneath them.

From a distance, I saw no sign of life around the huts, except the relentless whistling of birds, "stop, turn around," I ordered, the men simultaneously obeyed my order and I came face to face with them.

"Ruth, you can now hand over their guns back to them," I said, the three men looked at each other briskly before staring at me and without taking their eyes off me, "why do you trust us?" Mr. Spencer demanded, still holding the blood stained shirt firmly against his forehead to stem the bleeding, "I don't trust you my friends, trust no man born of a woman, I only need your help," I replied. The men stood motionless staring at me blankly with surprise boldly written on their faces, "George, take our guest to a nice room, while I get a better treatment, I will join you later," Spencer said flatly.

He turned back in company of frank and the two men walked towards the last huts to their extreme left Sir, George rubbing the back of his head, said, "please, do follow me to your room," He led I and Ruth to the second largest hut that was suspended about three feet above the ground. The stairs was made of neatly woven bamboo stem and looked strong enough to carry the weight of an ox.

The hut's tattered roof was further shaded by a big tree with vast branches, when we stepped inside the hut I got a different impression from the outside, the hut was beautifully furnished with cane sticks nicely woven into chairs, table shelf and bed. Beside the foam on the bed, most of the items in the hut were handmade, possibly from natural material. "Sir, feel at home here," George said spreading his arms out, I bowed to him as he walked pass me to the exit. When he closed the door, I looked at Ruth's glittering eyes. "Ruth, are you okay?" I asked, "no! Am very hungry," she replied, I walked up to her and placed my arms on her shoulder and my mind quickly raced to my beautiful Ajuma. "Sorry, I will find you what to eat," I said.

I went back inside and sat on the edge of the cane bed and laid my rifle on my lap while my finger encircled the trigger, George tapped on the door slightly before pushing it open. He placed a flat basket which served as a tray on the cane table, "Sir, this is our most cherished meal, commander said he will join you later," George said while revealing his multi colored tooth in a smile. "You mean Spencer?" I asked, "yes, Mr. Spencer, he is our commander here," he replied.

George took a few steps backward and left the room, I hastily laid my gun by the foot of the cane bed where I could reach it easily, and drew the table closer, Ruth hurriedly found a comfortable spot and sat down, I opened the largest clay bowl contained Oje-apka made from milled corn. The other bowl contained thick sticky soup, we ate together in silence without thinking we could be poisoned, being our first solid meal in days Ruth didn't spare any bit of the meal, after the meal Ruth cleared the bowl with her tongue.

A tap on the door made me reach for my rifle hurriedly, I quickly placed my right hand over the steel trigger of the gun without lifting it to view. When the door finally swung open, it turned out to be Spencer, accompanied by a strange young man. The man bowed to me and walked in patiently, and he urged Ruth to release the bowl she had already licked clean. I eased my grip on the trigger stood up and stretch my right hand for a hand shake that was immediately met by Spender's right hand. "Ruth! Ruth! Let go the bowl," I snapped. She quietly handed the waiting man the bowl and he looked at me sharply. The man left the hut with the empty bowls.

"I hope you enjoyed the meal," Spencer asked settling his buttocks on one of the cane chair, and he half sat and walked, dragging the chair closer to me. "I would like to wave an olive branch to you Mr. Reuben," he said calmly, you are a great material to behold," he paused briefly twisting his eye ball around in its socket, his eye balls reminded me of an owl, "your daughter can play outside while we talk," he continued. "it's not necessary Mr. Spencer, Ruth is my right hand baby, she will find out everything eventually soon or later," I replied, "that is alright then," he said adjusting himself in the chair. He gave details of his activities, and made me understand that there was plenty of money to be made from drug trade, especially his area of specialization, the Indian hemp.

When he was through with his analysis, I calculated the profit I stand to earn if I partake, could that open my way to Freetown?" I asked. Then he nodded, I also indicated my willingness to partake, so that I would be shown the way to Freetown to reunite with my colleagues, by the time Mr. Spencer left the hut, Ruth had slumped into a deep sleep. I helped align her to lay properly. I also decide to stretch out on the cane bed next to her.

I woke up the next morning when the sun's ray pierced through the raffia woven curtain. My eyes looked around, my sight first caught Ruth's sleep ridden body wide spread on the wooden floor, then my eyes zoomed to where I had left my automatic rifle and I found it was missing, I hurriedly searched the hut and found nothing. I was suspicious of the nature of sleep that knocked me out the previous night, I knew it was an extra ordinary kind of sleep, I later found out that the soup we ate the previous day had been stuffed with hemp.

All my efforts to wake Ruth up failed to bring her back to full state of consciousness, so I helped her to the bed and laid her on the bed properly. When I opened the door of the hut to my surprise, it opened without any hindrance, I came back and looked around the hut carefully and for anything unusual but found nothing in particular.

I slowly came out of the hut and headed to the next hut, I was half way to the hut when a voice ordered, "hold it there," I halted immediately and turned to see who the owner of the voice was, it turned out to be George's, he came out behind some rows of sand filled barrels shaded by tall grasses. "Mr. Reuben, you are prohibited from loitering around here without permission," he said, "forbidden? What for?" I asked, "please, save yourself from serious problem and return to your room now," When I hesitated, he shuffled a rifle and pointed it at me, that was when I realized he was carrying my rifle. Without altering a word, I went back to my room and laid on the bed staring blankly at the patchy roof.

Minutes turned into hours as I waited for the next incident, my ears were steadily engulfed by Ruth's whistling snore, my expectations ended when the door was pushed open by Mr. Spencer, flanked by two body guard, they entered the room. My eyes scanned both guards briskly, then my focus shifted to Ruth who was still asleep, "I must congratulate you Mr. Reuben for surviving the night," Spencer said, stretching his hand for a shake. I stared at the men without saying anything, "my men came here yesterday to stop you from breathing and to carry your baby away, but they were never allowed to do it. Something no one can explain stood on their way. I even tried to execute the task myself, but I saw what I never saw in my life," I listened to Spencer's tales with my lower lip almost falling off as it hung open, "I am here to commission you into our organization, if you don't mind," Spencer asked. I looked at the men thoughtfully. "My friends," I began, "I thank God for his protections," I paused briefly, I will play along with you but you will help me back to my base as soon as possible. I made the men under stood, I live a decent life style and would not propagate their own lifestyles and trade. I and Spencer discussed extensively until my meal and Ruth's was served, Spencer tasted the food to assure me of it safety before departing with his guards.

It took several minutes before I woke Ruth up, and it took even more time to get her to her senses. However the food on the table aided her recovery, we ate in silence and she went back to sleep moments after the meal.

Later at night, Spencer came into the hut alone, "how are you Mr. Reuben?" he asked? "I am alright" I replied, "let's go and get our boys ready for delivery, I have to get a hundred kilograms of hemp each to eight units of the rebel tonight," he said. "The orders are long overdue," he added, "while, it's alright if you don't mind," I replied.

He led the way out of the hut into the bushes, through a narrow path and we soon arrived at an open space surrounded by walls of dense shrubs. There we met fifteen men sitting on the ground and eight big sacks containing weeds laid on the ground close to them. The men spoke in low tone. I didn't quite understand what they were talking about.

"We want to get this across to the Rebels fighters on a regular basis even our customer comes from different background and organizations, we have various depots scattered across various border fronts." When I became overwhelmed with curiosity. I asked him what lectures the men were receiving, he smiled briefly and wrapped his arm around his chest, "They are learning how to insert drugs in different parts of their body, you can join the class if you feel like," Spencer said, "no, not yet please, I can't stand this yet," I said, "but that is how we earn our money," Spencer said and shrugged, "let's agree you make money but do you don't enjoy the money?" I asked, "I will, some days, when the wars around us comes to an end, one day," he replied, "but as long as men remain greedy and insatiable, they will always be war around us," I retorted.

I and Ruth stayed with Spencer in the jungle for about two weeks waiting for the opportunity to get back to my base join my Ecomog Peace Keeping Force. Spencer was very reluctant showing us our way to Freedom, instead he encouraged me to wait until some peace keepers come over to take their orders. I and Ruth accompanied Spencer to his weed farm as often as possible and Ruth ate well and seemed to be enjoying her stay.

One particular day when Spencer came to my hut to update me about what is going on the hemp plantation, I had to explain to him that I was not feeling alright, so before he left for his farm with Ruth that morning, he made some local herbs available for me and promised the herbs will make me feel alright again. I reluctantly allowed Ruth follow Spencer to his plantation, hoping it would help me get extra sleep.

I administered the herbs as Spencer had previously prescribed. Moments later my bowel knew some peace again and I soon fell as sleep afterward, I didn't know how long I slept before an outburst of gunfire erupted outside jolting me out of my cane bed. The intensity of the gun fire clearly indicated that a fierce battle was going on outside. Without hesitation, I laid flat on the suspended wooden floor of the hut. The morning was still premature and I wondered where Ruth was and if she was safe. I prayed the raiders should turn out to be Ecomog fighters. Moments later I saw a bright glow of flame outside. I became more frightened when I realized a hut had been set ablaze. Occasionally bullets pierced the fragile wooden walls of my hut and because no fire was returned from my hut, it got very little barrage of shots, but the resistance from the huts had been almost subdued, and the second hut went up in flame, I quickly realized that laying on the floor was becoming the wrong move to make at this point. I hurriedly put on a sandal and waited briefly. The intensity of the gun fire clearly indicated fierce fighting was going on outside without hesitation, I laid flat on the suspended wooden floor of the hut, the morning was still premature, I wondered where Ruth was then, and if she was safe.

I prayed that the raiders should turn out to be Ecomog troops, so that my Freedom would come at last. Each passing moment saw the fighting growing fiercer. Moments later, I saw a bright low flame outside, I became more frightened when I realized my hut had been set ablaze. I crawled to one side of the wall and peeped outside. Sweat began trickling down my forehead. The people I saw outside made my breath seize. I saw four RUF rebels from my angle of view laid ambush outside and fully armed. I carefully crawled to the four corners of the hut and I saw the entire camp had been encircled and being razed down by the RUF rebel.

With the aid of my desperation to survive, I managed to pull a couple of wood off the floor of the hut which was already partially on fire, I carefully lowered myself between the wooden floor, I concealed myself under the floor where I had better view of the battle field, the fire that caught the hut raged but it miraculously didn't consume the floor of the hut where I hid myself, but the heat from the fire almost forced me out to the waiting hands of the ruthless RUF rebels.

When guns became silent again, the rebels had successfully over ran the hideout. I had someone ran near my partially burnt out hut and sprayed several shot inside the remnant of the burnt out hut and one of the bullet narrowly missed my shoulder by an inch. When he was convinced no one was inside, I heard his footsteps leave the hut.

My entire mind was submerged in great fear of uncertainty I prayed to God to save my endangered soul, Although I quivered, I had a feeling within me that God's always at work for my sake and that I will never be subdued. Miraculous all the rebels moved out of the side of the hut. I heard orders been issued out by a very familiar voice, I recognized to be General Mosquito's commanders I had previously worked with, I was close to them then so I was able to recognize some of the rebels.

The earlier I escaped form here the better for me, I thought, as soon as I was sure the rebels had moved out of my side of the hut, I carefully commenced pulling out the barriers that formed walls around the base of the hut to make way for my escape. It took me a few minutes to create enough room for my body to sneak through the space I had created.

'' Lulu, can't be deceptive, I believe he saw Reuben here, comb every inch of this hide out immediately, he might be hiding somewhere," the familiar commander's voice barked. I ignored the order, I suddenly surged out of hiding into the open and ran as fast as I could for my life. The rattling of machine gun fire immediately rented the air almost forcing me to surrender but a strange supernatural force propelled me on, keeping my head as low as I could, I found myself dashing deep into the forest like a virgin stallion. The burden of running without a rifle gave me an advantage over the furious rebels chasing me. Having no apparent knowledge of where my spirit would land me. I; prayed in my heart for God's guardians and protection, God didn't fail me, I was chased into the jungle for about thirty minutes by the rebels. When I finally decided to pause for extra oxygen, it was then I realized I had successfully shaken off the rebels off my trail.

I slumped to my knee and supported my shoulder with both hands on the ground. Mass of air gushed in and out of my lung, Moments later, I felt my shirt was clinging to my skin. When I looked at myself, I realized I had been hit by a bullet on my right shoulder. Without hesitation, I unbutton my shirt and pulled it below where the shot had caught me and with the help of a sharp stick, I fumbled through the open wound on my shoulder carefully and saw where the bullet was lodged, I carefully pulled the bullet out of my body. I was grateful the bullet had not severed any of my vertebra, I only suffered a big flesh wound.

I crushed the tip of the bullet I removed from my body with a piece of rock and I poured part of the bullet powder on the bleeding wound and I also squeezed some leaves to paste and spread the juice on the wound. Miraculously, the bleeding subsided.

When I got up to continue, the prickling pain under my foot pulled me back to my knee. The slippers-like sandal I wore before my escape had attracted various thorns, it took me about five minutes to get rid of all the thorns, and I was able to set out again. The morning sunlight shone greatly, striking me each time the vegetation failed to shield me, and birds whistled hilariously on tree tops with no qualms.

I knew I would never leave the area without rescuing Ruth. So I used my initiatives to navigate the jungle in search of Ruth. As minutes ticked by I felt my strength eluding me, I searched for my way to the plantation for several hours, my search got a boost when I spotted an Iroko tree that served as our rest spot on our way to and from the hemp plantation, the Iroko tree also served as a yardstick to guide the extent of our trips, very cautiously. I started tracing my way to the plantation with the help of the trees position, when I finally got into the hemp plantation I was surprised by the calmness that greeted me. The only sounds that vibrated into my ears were sonorous songs of birds and winds rattling the vegetation. I approached the plantation cautiously from a difficult area and refusing to step into the open. I cycled a quarter of the plantation without seeing any sign of Ruth. I became more worried and confused, having no idea of Ruth's wellbeing turned me completely sad.

I continued my search around praying to find Ruth before the RUF rebels find her. A sudden blast of shot jerked my pause rate abruptly, I dived to the base of a nearby tree for cover and waited to be sure of the source of the shot, I heard the shot echo in the distance and the cry of a female voice followed, I immediately recognized it was Ruth, I got out of hiding and cautiously walked toward the direction of the cry. When I got there, I saw Ruth carrying an AK47 pointed at a man lying lifelessly on the ground, "Ruth!" I called. Another wild shot rang out in response to my call. I quickly dived into the nearest vegetation for cover, thinking she had become possessed by her strange visitor.

When I called her three times again, she dropped the rifle and ran to embrace me in tears, I hurriedly got to my feet on time to get hold of her as she crushed into my chest. I hugged her, and whispered some soothing word into her ears. "He wanted to force me," Ruth said amid tears. "He tried to tie me to a big wood, that wood," she said pointing to a big log lying on the ground beside the lifeless body of a man. "It's alright now, I am with you," I said, she withdrew from my embrace. When she suddenly saw my terrible bullet wound, "what is this?" she asked, "who did it to you Daddy?" She continued without giving me the option to brew an answer to her first question, I shrugged, and tried to give her a short explanation. Suddenly, rattling of automatic gun fire pulled me off my relaxed mood and another round of life race was flagged off.

The more I tried to run faster the more I realized my strength was dwindling. The gun battle grew fierce in the distance but I had no idea who the rebels were battling. I was forced to stop and relax to gain some fresh strength to run again, "Ruth where did Spencer go?" I asked, ''he went back home with some men when we saw smoke in the sky and heard machine gun fire. She concluded, he must be the one clashing with the rebels, I thought.

A few minutes later, we started out again, but this time much slower. Knowing that danger was a little further away, and each time I stopped to run and let in more air into my lung, it was as if I was not getting enough oxygen, and with my fast depleting strength, getting medical treatment remained paramount to my continuous existence. Ruth was very worried about my state, she held my left hand to her chest tightly as if I was at the verge of dying. We soon sighted a stream and a big thirst sapped my throat. I quickly knelt beside the pool of water and with my hand I sipped the water slowly avoiding swallowing insects and leaves by the whiskers. Ruth also joined me and we both drank together. I remembered sipping thrice when an external violent forces pushed me from behind sending me somersaulting into the stream.

As I struggled to gain my bearing, I heard Ruth's loud cry. The cry helped to energized and sharpen my mental state, I actualized my sight while still in the water. I saw a soldiers standing by the stream grabbing Ruth by her right arm. The man was well above six feet and had the chest of a bear. He kept staring at me as I struggled to gain my balance in the stream, the quail expression on Ruth's face told me the unfolding incident was not pleasant to Ruth's imagination, I poked my hands into the bed of the stream as if I was trying to balance myself and scooped a handful of sand an threw it at the man's face, as he bent to avoid the missile, he lost his center of gravity when Ruth struggled to break loose. With the slight opportunity I jumped out of the pool early enough to land my right punch on his left jaw, the impact of the punch sent him to his knees, and his grip broke off Ruth's arm. She quickly stepped away from the man as I swung a left kick at the soldier, he manage to grab my leg and I hopped like a Kangaroo to balance my weight, but he jerked the captured leg, thus making nonsense of my effort, I landed on the ground with a thud, before I could craw to my feet the man was already over me, when his first punch landed on my jaw, I felt like millions of brightly colored stars exploded in my eyes, when the second punch caught my head, I felt the man was using a steel coated fist to hit me. I grabbed his third punch with my right hand, and he tried to hit me with his left fist I grabbed it as well, he struggled to break loose and before he could. Ruth struck him with a stick on his head, the impact made him lost his strength briefly which gave me the privilege to overpower him. When I finally did, I got to my feet and moved quickly to strike him with my feet, but the impact of a rifle butt struck me behind my head violently and I suddenly became unconscious.

I woke up the next morning and looked around sharply to be sure of where I was, Ruth's smiling face greeted me, "Daddy," she called, "your friends are good people," she explained. I was dumb founded and only looked around, the white bandage on my shoulder reminded me of the past, and very rapidly the past events came back to light in my memory. Very little of the many exciting stories of her experience since she arrived here got my reception, but she succeeded in talking me to sleep.

Somehow I woke up that evening feeling much more conscious and better, I strolled around to acquaint myself with the vicinity. After my fight with that soldier, he turned out to be an Ecomog soldier, his colleagues stepped in to assist him during our fight. It was at that point I was struck down by one of his colleagues with the butt of his rifle. I was later identified as a missing in action soldier when I was brought to Ecomog base and I got the best medical attention available there.

I saw Ruth at the entrance of the health Centre looking very joyful, she ran and embraced me and then grabbed my hand. "Ruth, thank God you are happy now," I said, she looked at me and smiled. The numbers of patient in very critical condition in the wards would force tears out of any eyes. I and Ruth took a walk around hand in hand round the Health Center vicinity. Every minute in my heart I remain thankful to God for saving me.

I decided I should see Nancy and her mother, that evening, so I and Ruth went there together. I was shocked when I found out that Nancy and her mother had vacated where they used to occupy. I looked around the area and beckoned a small boy around playing his self-made toy, "Do you know Nancy who used to live here with her mother?" I asked. "I know, Aunty Nancy, the boy replied. "Where is she now?" I asked "I don't know, some soldiers came to move her away with her mother," he replied, on hearing that I paid no more attention to the boy's other comment, "alright boy, thank you I said." I took Ruth to my bed bunk, I once again saw my bunk bed after many months in the jungle, I was congratulated by some of my colleagues that were present then with a loud cheer, I quickly summarized their solidarity visits and made sure Ruth had something to eat.

After our meal together, I said "I will like to visit some friends of mine in down town." She looked curiously at me and pleaded "Daddy, please I will like to go with you," Ruth insisted, "you need a lot of rest, you have to eat and sleep," I said, I was able to convince her to stay back. While I pleaded with a colleague to keep her company.

I then started the search for Nancy, then the sun had begun its final journey for the day and the ruined state of Freetown hadn't changed a bit. After a long walk I finally got to the ramshackle that used to be the home of Nancy and her mother before I relocated them to the Ecomog safe camp.

As I approached the entrance my heart raced in curiosity, the narrow corridor was without any luminous source. My feet stuck an object and I stumbled and almost fell. After the accompanying noise subsided, I listened for any human response and there was none I then walked up to the cupboard that shielded the entrance to their only shelter and tapped it softly and waited, there was no response, I did it thrice and I got no response still, I then became impatient and decided to move the cupboard myself, my hands were barely on the cupboard when a chill steel touched the back of my neck. A big chill crawled up my spine and I stood still, "your hands up," a sonorous feminine voice echoed. I quickly obeyed the order, "who are you?" The voice asked, at that point I realized it was Nancy. "Nancy!" I called, "its Reuben, and stop harassing me please," I said, "Reuben! Is that you?"

She grabbed me and almost lifted me off my feet, the pressure she exerted on my shoulder made me yell out in pain. When I was finally able to face her she kissed and bit my lip softly. "Nancy, why are you here?" I asked in other to restrain her from showing more emotion, she then busted out sobbing before she could say anything further, she fought back tears and deep emotion to explain what she and her mother had been encountering. She explained that ever since she had been spotted by my commandant the day she came to look for me, she had never known peace. Her mother was thrown out of the camp one night for no just reason. I tried to console her, after while she took me in to meet her mother.

I kept them company for about an hour during which I briefly narrated my ordeal in the hands of the RUF rebels. When I finally decided it's time to go back, Nancy insisted I pass the night with them. "Reuben, you have to stay to keep I and mama happy again after this long nightmare without you," she urged. Her mother had slipped into a deep sleep during the course of my story, I explained how impossible it is to leave Ruth alone to pass the night, and the consequences that await my violation of laid down military rules, and after I had repeatedly assured her that I would return the next day as soon as possible and possibly with Ruth, she then reluctantly accompanied me for about three minutes which took us to a road intersection, and after a few moments of what I considered a speech rehearsal I prevailed on her to return home to her mother.

Darkness had enveloped the entire atmosphere and coupled with the total blackout in Freetown, it depicts a vivid picture of a ghost town in all ways it is viewed. I hurriedly made my way through the deserted street to beat the curfew time.

I arrived my bunk bed to find Ruth already snoring in a deep sleep, "Reuben, thank God you are back, your little baby has been worried," Lance corporal Okon said, Okon was a fellow soldier and part of the peace keeping contingent, with a smallish frame but his old brush-like mustache always gave out his age. He was the one I pleaded with to keep Ruth Company while I was away. "I hope she didn't bug you much?" I asked. "Not really, I enjoyed her curiosity," Okon answered flatly. Just then Sgt Abdullahi, the man behind our battalion's signal affairs walked in, "Hey! Awoha," he greeted. We responded to his compliment in similar manner, he then brought out a brown envelope from his hip pocket, "Rueben, this letter came in from Nigeria last Tuesday," he said, and he handed it to me, "thank you sir, I said. I stood at attention briefly in a military styled salutation, he turned and left immediately. Okon saw the eagerness boldly written all over me as I ignored him and struggled with shaky hands to open the letter, when I finally did, I satisfied my curiosity about who wrote the letter, Ajuma.

Ajaja Military Cantonment,
Apapa Lagos. Nigeria
7/11/98

Dear Husband,

It's being quite a while since heard from you, I am sure you are alive and in good health because I always see you in my dreams, I understand it's not easy finding time to write in the kind of situation you are in Sierra-lone.

My plight and guilt has eaten my heart up and I know I will die if I don't tell you what I am encountering, I am pregnant under an ugly circumstances. I don't know who to blame.

My welfare got so bad as a result of my inability to secure the money you said I will be getting monthly. I have not been able to get a kobo ever since. In order to survive I resulted to selling roasted plantain at our bus stop.

One fateful day my wares and the entire money I made was taken away from me by some uniformed men claiming to be clearing the street of street traders. I lost all I had in that incident, so hunger and starvation took the worst turn for me.

I then approached your uncle to loan me the capital to start another trade. After weeks of pleading, he brought me dangerously too close to him. On that fateful day he assured me I would get the money the next day so he bought me a fruit drink I became unconscious after drinking the fruit juice. When I regained consciousness again, I found myself naked on the bed.

Now I am pregnant, and knowing fully well that you were receiving fertility treatment. When we were together, I feel I am carrying a bastard.

I am not begging for your forgiveness, I am seriously considering suicide to rest my young soul. May God be with you always, whatever becomes of my fate you will always be my only love.

Yours Ajuma.

The letter dropped from my hand, I became completely disoriented and devastated, I looked around me and found I was alone beside Ruth that was miles away in sleep.

I knelt down beside Ruth, closing my eyes and fist tightly, I made a fervent vow to avenge all that were behind I and Ajuma's plight's including the military..............

A LOOK AT AFRICA'S PLIGHT IN THE HANDS OF ITS LEADERS

I grew up as a little boy in Idah, a middle belt state of Kogi State, Nigeria, A fairly large ancient town, the town is more or less an Island, surrounded by River Niger and a yellowish coloured stream called INNACHALO. The stream runs almost across the entire town, yet the town's inhabitants find it extremely difficult to get access to portable drinking water.

The same fact applies to the continent of Africa, Africa is home to abundant human and natural resources that translates to trillions of US dollar in monetary value. Yet the inhabitants of the continent can only showcase the poorest sets of humans, dilapidated infrastructure and a comatose economics on our dear planet earth.

Since the emancipation of Africa and the proliferation of independence and self-governance on the continent, Africa has never known real peace. It is therefore apparent that the continent is plagued by a powerful widespread elite ideology, corruption, embezzlement, craze for power, political instability etc. and the subsequent refusal of the very few but powerful section of its citizenry to fully abide by the constituted norms for an equitable and selfless governance on the continent.

It is very unfortunate to note that all the geo-political sections of the continent are at different stages of conflict and attrition thereby setting the entire continent on an inextinguishable flame of deadly blood bath which had so far claimed millions of human lives and cost trillions of US dollars in monetary value.

Well over 65 percent of African rulers opt for violence at the slightest provocation to settle disputes that arise during their stay in power. Because of the astronomical high rate of unemployment and poverty on the continent, just for pea-nuts, jobless youths are easily cajoled by selfish rulers to spill the blood of their fellow countrymen and with the easy availability of hard drugs, such innocent youths are in no time transformed into wild murderers, maiming machines, rapists and destroyers.

It is however sad to learn that Africa has committed over 65 percent of her wealth to sponsoring destructive conflicts of various dimensions in the past. Zimbabwe for instance, spent over 30 million US dollars monthly on backing the military operation of Democratic Republic of Congo's (D.R.C) ruler, President Laurent Kabila against the insurgence in the east of the country, while its citizen die of hunger, curable diseases and extreme poverty. President Yowere Museveni of Uganda and former President Pascal Bizimungu of Rwanda committee much more of their countries' hard earned wealth and human live backing the Congolese rebels to dethrone President Laurent Kabila. Thereby setting the stage for a proxy war among member nations of regional body.

When Charles Taylor, Mohammed Farra, and Jonas Savembi took up arms against their respective governments the world was fooled by their mouthwatering purported intensions, but as their conflicts grew fiercer by the day claiming hundreds of thousands of innocent lives, properties and state infrastructures, the international community was thrown into confusion about the aftermath of the war that posed the threat of wiping out the entire populace of those countries. In Liberia Sierra Leone alone, the Nigeria government committed millions of US dollars daily including human lives in form of troops to reinstate normalcy in those country. Hard earned financial resource that would have been spent on infrastructural development and improving the standard of living of the citizens, such fund were instead used to destroy lives and properties.

In Angola, the former top cold war opponents (U.S.A and former U.S.S.R) showcased their military powers in support of National Union for the Total Independence of Angola (UNITA) rebels and the Angola government respectively, to prove a point that bears no regard for human lives.

We should therefore never be impressed by any violent Messiah with claims of getting rid of corrupt and wayward Leaders to institute credible reform in government. These are always their claims in order to attract underserved favours from their people and the international communities.

From the slitting of innocent throat in the Middle East, to the inhuman amputation of limbs in West Africa especially in Sierra-Leone by the Revolutionary United Front (RUF) rebels and others, it's like a wave of violent madness soaring on the continent. Today's generation of African rulers have achieved nothing but crisis on the continent, they have therefore failed woefully as leaders. There is need for total repentance among African rulers from their self-centered attitudes.

The evil and violent attitudes of some African rulers are being copied and adopted by youths in their various institutions of learning for example. The proliferation of various dreaded secret cults in Nigeria's institutions of learning which has made life miserable for the peace loving inhabitants of the society. The evil activities of this secret occult has led to the death of thousands of brilliant and ambitious students since their inception.

The then famine stricken people of the Horn of Africa, expected their respective governments to provide relief of all kinds to allay their fears of dying of hunger and curable disease. Instead President Isaias Afwerki and his Ethiopian Counterpart president Menes Zenawi both of Ethiopia and Eritrea opted to spend several hundreds of millions of US dollars waging a senseless war against each other over a piece of land that is not arable and is believed to contain no mineral resources.

Hundreds of millions of US dollar was wasted by both rulers, including lives of youths that would have contributed to the future development of both countries, the aftermath of the crises brought about the neglect of the plights of their people, thereby leaving them at the mercy of international humanitarian organizations and donor countries.

Recently, women in Rwanda, Burundi and Somalia in their desperate search for spouses resolved to getting married to much older men, and there were men marrying six or more wives due to the lack of young men of marriageable age, most of whom have lost their lives in the senseless war in their respective countries.

The wave of violent madness soaring across Africa has made the people of the continent the most impoverished humans on earth. I believe the continent has not learnt enough to be self-governing. A great mistake was made by the colonial Masters by granting some Africa countries premature independence, their actions has committed some Africa countries to the hands of very few untamed dictators whose lust for power are insatiable and their thirst for wealth are unparalleled, and the very few outstanding rulers of Africa are sometimes polluted by these selfish rulers of unimaginable proportion.

President Charles Taylor of Liberia who was the ruler of the oldest independent nation in Africa was no doubt the greatest security nightmare of the West African sub-region. After the dark days of the Liberia civil war, the greatest cruelty of the war was credited to President Taylor's National Patriotic Front of Liberia (N.P F.L) Rebels. He is also believed to be busy fueling the Sierra-Leonean civil war by backing the R.U.F rebels logistically and otherwise in exchange for diamonds in the rebel controlled areas of Sierra-Leone, President Taylor is alleged to be also harming innocent civilians including children who were not from his tribe

The Liberian president's belief in violence and his policies of using Liberia's hard earned wealth to ferment trouble, human suffering and death in the West African sub-region is most uncivilized and is a display of sheer lunacy.

Since the dethronement and arrest of Charles Tailor and his subsequent trial and conviction in the International Court of Justice, the entire west Africa sub region has been void of civil war, the region now enjoy relative calm. Therefore, there is every reason to believe that certain power-drunk individuals are profiting from other people's plight.

If it's not greed, selfishness and absolute madness, how else would one describe men who for decades continuously tighten their grips on power. Most of these African tyrants do not even possess a proper educational qualification to govern a primary school and lack all moral qualities to head a family but are today through the barrel of guns rulers of nations and even the continent of Africa.

Names like President Gnassingbe Eyadema of Togo who is credited for staging the first popular Coup de tat on the continent on January 13th 1963 whose son succeeded his father after his death is reminiscent of the dragon in the biblical revelation. A leader with blood on his hands.

President Eyadema has pioneered self-imposition on the continent and has crushed fellow contestants with resounding military force and rulers like, Ibrahim Mainassara (Niger), Idi Amin (Uganda), Blaise Compaore (Burkino faso), Sani Abacha (Nigeria), Robert Mugabe (Zimbabwe) and others have happily embraced the evil status of president Eyadema.

Today's Africa is been colonized by Africans in the most brutal manner shocking to even the continents old colonial masters.

It was greatly disheartening when UNHCR presented a report about the animalistic abuse of Burundian women and Children refugees in refugee camps in Tanzania, where one in every four women and girls have been rapped. The report detailed how innocent and defenseless Burundians women and girls were being rapped, violently abused and deprived the right to survive. In the UNHCR's recommendation on how to find a lasting solution to the dilemma, the agency could only recommend that women should stop going to fetch firewood and that money should be made available to the Tanzanian police to protect the women. Does Tanzanian police need special fund to discharge their primary responsibility in the society of protecting the lives and properties of the inhabitants of Tanzania and indeed of defenseless refuges?

None of the recommendations made any sense, the UNHCR failed to make a strong statement against the barbaric rebels exploits that led to the vulnerability of the women and children to violent and sexual attacks. UNHCR is in a position to make statements and recommendations that are realistic and are able to influence drastic action against the rebels' inhuman exploits.

President of Burundi is a happy and comfortable man, so are the rebel leaders of all the various rebel groups that are busy engineering humanitarian disaster in Burundi and its environs. The international community and African rulers must be able to enforce peace in troubled nation on the continent and if not, the over 750,000 million Africans must see it as a necessity to enforce peace on their continent, by refusing to pick up arms against ourselves just because of a politician

The security challenges presently confronting the region now is global in nature, Islamic radicalism is a global crisis, and it's been forth across many front on a global scale, the region has not been an exception, from the al Qaida in the Islamic Maghreb operating in north Africa including Mali, to the dreaded Boko Haram sect operating in some parts of Northern Nigeria, Niger, Chad and Cameroon.

WAY FORWARD

Achieving stability and peace on the continent of Africa requires collective actions from all quarters against the continent's evil rulers. The People of Africa must wake up and reshape their destiny for good; it's a matter of choice and work. No ruler should be allowed to offer its citizens a drop of water in exchange for their blood. If the blood shed on the continent is scoped into a container, it's no doubt going to form the first sea of blood in the world enough to drown all the evil perpetrators in the planet, yet some African rulers are eager to shed other people's blood for their political ambition, while doing everything possible to safeguard themselves and members of their family.

Crisis management Ambassadors (representatives) should be appointed by the United Nation Organization to all countries of the continent to carefully monitor events that could lead to security challenges as they unfold in their countries of assignment and to alert the world body on modalities for quelling such emerging crisis before they get out of control.

Stiff embargo must be clamped on all warring countries of Africa by the international community to stem their military capabilities. This will proof the international community's genuine commitment to assisting the continent. I believe it's time for the world to suspend indefinitely sales of military hardware to all African countries because wars are not possible without weapons. Money saved from the defense spending can be re-injected into the economy of the continent.

All trouble brewing rulers of Africa must be shown the way out by the UN with strict policies formulate and enacted by the UN and other concerned bodies for that purpose. There must be no abode for evil minded rulers on the continent and indeed the entire world.

Industrial actions have proven very effective in bending many stiff government policies. I strongly believe Africans must adopt industrial actions against any of their governments that want to drag them into war to settle self-inspired disputes. Peace must be maintained in Africa before the battle against poverty and diseases can be won on the continent. The greatest war every African should be fighting is the war against AIDS, malaria, hunger, deadly and curable diseases, poverty etc. The continent's wealth must be invested in order to alleviate the plights of Africans.

The African Union (AU) and the United Nations Organization should establish an institution for peace (PEACE AND LEADERSHIP INSTITUTE OF AFRICA) where African rulers must attend periodically to learn peacemaking, leadership norms, economic policies, true leadership.

Whoever is standing for the mantle of leadership in Africa must have his personal accounts frozen at home and abroad during his tenure and should only be left with one account that can easily be monitored to curb the embezzlement of public funds that may later be used against the masses to stir crisis that could lead to war. One of the primary problem confronting the continent of Africa is poverty, Deadly conflicts and the greed of some rulers on the continent are the major forces behind the abject poverty in Africa despite its enormous God endowed natural resources.

Africa Peace Media (APM) should be establish across the continent by the UN and AU to propagate peace and developmental ideas across the continent through radio, television and print Medias. The A.P.M should be empowered and run by veterans of all fields of human endeavors to broadcast across the continent like other media organizations, e.g. BBC, VOA etc. through the medias, youths can easily be advise to shun any violent preaching messiah and youths would learn not to accept drops of water in exchange for their precious blood from such leaders. The medium should create a forum for embittered and aggrieved rulers and their opponents to come and iron out their differences in the open. Where the public can easily call on phone or otherwise to stress their concerns.

Because of the evil tendencies of some African rulers, they shield themselves in an enclosure of luxury, thereby making interaction difficult with the people they are governing. The Africa peace media project will go a long way in tearing down the shield that protect African rulers from the cries of their people.

Nigeria has God Almighty to thank for its peace and tension soaked stability, despite of all the intimidation and aggression over the years. Hence the country's refusal to be plunged into another civil war. After giving God the credit, Nigeria's systematic distribution of wealth that has seen virtually all ethnic groups of the country having comfortable and self-styled millionaires and achievers with enormous properties and businesses to protect, plays an important role in discouraging any act of wide spread violence and destruction of properties in Nigeria.

Extreme neglect of some ethnic groups do spark off violent reactions and are actually the causes of most conflicts in Africa. Tribalism and nepotism must be discouraged on the continent and an equitable distribution of state wealth and power should always be encouraged to prevent dangerous and volatile agitations.

English language is being thought in all levels of the educational system which enable billions of humans to communicate in English language worldwide. PEACE should be developed into a simplified educational subject universally and thought in all levels of our educational system. It will go a long way in addressing violence in our schools that are later carried over to work places and possible leadership positions. The young generation must be thought the pattern of peace from infancy so they don't depart from it when they grow old.

The next generation of Africans must not slip into the same mistake of the present day Africans. The most cost effective solution to any problem is prevention and early dialogue.

When a man is fed with honey for too long, he will regard water's taste as bitter. The duration of military service by individuals should be reduced in Africa to minimize the long grip on top military posts by certain individuals or ethnic groups before he get carried away by the intoxicating effects of power and wealth associated with the positions. This will allow others the opportunity to serve their father land, thereby allowing equitable distribution of military opportunities.

The clamor for African renaissance must be taken seriously with lot of creative initiatives for a sustainable growth for all beneficial aspects of the continent. Religious fanaticism plays a great role in crisis generation and fueling in Africa. For over two decades the Muslim dominated north of Sudan battled rebels in the Christian and Animist dominated south, hundreds of thousands of lives has been lost and billions of US Dollars had also been flushed down the drain in the senseless conflict.

The most diverse populous black nation on earth, Nigeria, whose northern part of the country is busy adopting strict Islam law (Sharia) thus making Islam an official religion of the affected states. The action has sparked series of violent unrest claiming thousands of lives and properties worth millions of US Dollars, and has further giving birth to the dreaded Boko Haram Islamic sect.

The AU should formulate a workable policy to make it illegal for any section of a state on the continent to declare any religion a state religion.

It is unfortunate that AU is worst off in weakness than a clawless, peak less and wingless eaglet. The document that brought the African most reformed organization to existence lack the merit to make the organization an accomplished and successful body like NATO and the European Union. There is therefore need for a complete reformation of the African Union. So the body can be legally and otherwise equipped to face the present day changes and challenges on the continent. The weakness of the AU has contributed a great deal to the sidelining of the entire continent globally. The loose association between the member nations of the body has made the continent most vulnerable to foreign manipulations which is detrimental to the success and advancement of the continent.

It is greatly disheartening when UNHCR presented a report about the animalistic abuse of Burundian women and Children refugees in refugee camps in Tanzania, where one in every four women and girls have been rapped. The report detailed how innocent and defenseless Burundians women and girls were being rapped, violently abused and deprived the right to survive. In the UNHCR's recommendation on how to find a lasting solution to the dilemma, the agency could only recommend that women should stop going to fetch firewood and that money should be made available to the Tanzanian police to protect the women. Does Tanzanian police need special fund to discharge their primary responsibility in the society of protecting the lives and properties of the inhabitants of Tanzania and indeed of defenseless refuges?

None of the recommendations made any sense, the UNHCR failed to make a strong statement against the barbaric rebels exploits that led to the vulnerability of the women and children to violent and sexual attacks. UNHCR is in a position to make statements and recommendations that are realistic and are able to influence drastic action against the rebels' inhuman exploits.

President of Burundi is a happy and comfortable man, so are the rebel leaders of all the various rebel groups that are busy engineering humanitarian disaster in Burundi and its environs. The international community and African rulers must be able to enforce peace in troubled nation on the continent and if not, the over 750,000 million Africans must see it as a necessity to enforce peace on their continent, by refusing to pick up arms against ourselves just because of a politician

Printed in the United States
By Bookmasters